Turning ™

Points

4

Communicating in English

Giuliano Iantorno / Mario Papa

ADDISON-WESLEY PUBLISHING COMPANY

Reading, Massachusetts • Menlo Park, California • New York
Don Mills, Ontario • Wokingham, England • Amsterdam
Bonn • Sydney • Singapore • Tokyo • Madrid • San Juan

A Publication of the World Language Division

Developmental Editors: Talbot Hamlin, Jennifer Bixby, Claire Smith, Ann Strunk

Production/Manufacturing: James W. Gibbons

Photo Research: Merle Sciacca

Consultants
Robert Saitz   Charles Skidmore

Design, production and illustration provided by Publishers' Graphics, Inc., Bethel, Connecticut. Artists: Marie DeJohn, S. D. Schindler, Joel Snyder

Cover design by Marshall Henrichs

Acknowledgments

We want to express our appreciation to the staff of the World Language Division of Addison-Wesley for all their efforts to make this series a reality. From the inception of the program, Robert Naiva, Executive Vice-President, and Judith Bittinger, Vice President and Editor-in-Chief, lent their enthusiasm and understanding to the methodology and philosophy of the course. To them, to Charles Skidmore for his many contributions to this book, and to the editors who prepared the manuscripts for publication, including Jennifer Bixby, Talbot Hamlin, Claire Smith and Ann Strunk, we extend our warmest thanks.

Giuliano Iantorno

Mario Papa

Photographs: Access Productions, Kevin McKiernan, 111; American Foundation for the Blind, 61, 62, 63; Art Resources, 48, 51, 54, 55, 56; Jack Bailey Studio, 29 center; Lorraine Bonney, 74, 76; Courtesy of Digital Equipment Corporation, 41 top and bottom L, 43 center, 45; Ford Motor Company, 41 center L; Gallaudet College, 60; The Image Bank, 104; Bobby Noel Kramer, 41 top R, 43 bottom; Lawrence Eagle Tribune, 43 top; The Erwin E. Smith Collection of the Library of Congress on deposit at the Amon Carter Museum, 27 bottom L; Mary E. Messenger, 97; Metropolitan Opera, New York, 82; Movie Star News, 83, 101, 115 bottom L; Courtesy of the Museum of Transportation, Brookline, MA, 105; NASA, all photos, 115, except bottom L; National Climatic Data Center, Asheville, NC, 21; National Portrait Gallery, 88 bottom R; Department of Commerce/NOAA/NESDIS, 20; Palomar Observatory Photographs, 117, 118; Peabody Museum, 88 top, 90; Original artwork by John Richard Perry, 73; Philadelphia City Council, 112; Popperfoto, London, 70 L; ProRodeo Cowboys Association, 27 top R and L, 29 top and bottom; Courtesy of the Rockwell Kent Legacies, 88 bottom L, 89; Salem Evening News, 69; Claire Smith, 59, 85; *Ocean Liners of the Past, Olympic and Titanic*, published by Patrick Stephens Ltd., Thorsons Publishing Group, England, 70 R; Kenneth Springer, 27 bottom R; Steinway and Sons, 84 center, 88 bottom; Texas Tourist Development Agency, Michael Murphy, 27 top center; Ralph P. Turcotte, Jr., 84 bottom L; Wideworld Photos, 34; Woods Hole Oceanographic Institute, 41 bottom R; Yerkes Primate Research Center and Georgia State University, 38.

Special acknowledgment is made to Trisha Geiger (Customer Service) and Dick Brandt (Photographer) of Webcrafters, Inc., Madison, WI, for their help with pages 91-2.

ISBN 0-201-06324-7
ISBN 0-201-52160-1 School Spec. Ed.
DEFGHIJKLMN-WC-99876543210

CONTENTS

* Words and music to the songs are in the Teacher's Guide.

* Words and music to the songs are in the Teacher's Guide.

* Words and music to the songs are in the Teacher's Guide.

1 TEENAGERS TODAY

Carlos Ramos is a young journalist who has recently joined the news staff at Channel 8 television. Today he is showing his friend Barbara around the station.

CARLOS: We do our panel shows here in Studio 2.

BARBARA: What's this group going to talk about?

CARLOS: They're going to talk about teenagers and their relationships. That's Jean MacPherson, our news director. We can watch it from the control room.

JEAN: Welcome to "Teenagers Today," brought to you by Channel 8 News. I'm Jean MacPherson. Our guests today are John Moreno, Diane Wang, and Steve Robinson. John, who has already been on this program, is a junior in high school.

JOHN: That's right. And I'm 17 years old.

JEAN: And what about you, Diane?

DIANE: I'm 18 and a senior. I was born in Hong-Kong but I've been here since I was five.

JEAN: Steve?

STEVE: I'm a junior, like John, and I'm 16.

JEAN: Today we're talking about getting along with other people. Diane, will you start?

DIANE: Well, I think that first you have to deal with the relationships in your own family.

JEAN: You think the family's pretty basic.

DIANE: Yes, I do. My parents love me—but things aren't always as easy as they look.

JEAN: You find it's difficult, sometimes, talking with them?

DIANE: Well, they just don't talk about feelings very much. It's as if they're afraid to. I haven't gotten through to them yet.

JOHN: But teenagers who don't talk to their parents can wind up with some serious problems. We need to know our parents will listen to us and take us seriously.

STEVE: That's right. Parents should listen to their children more. And we should try to understand what it feels like to be them!

JEAN: Thank you, we'll be back in a minute with more about teenagers and their feelings.

Communication Points
Ask and talk about feelings and relationships

Diane, Steve, and John feel that teenagers and their parents need to talk more about feelings. Here are some other points about which they might have talked. Read each of the statements and decide which of them you agree with and which you disagree with. On your paper, write the number of the statement, the word AGREE or DISAGREE, and one or two sentences telling why you agree or disagree with it. Then discuss the statements with your partner.

1. Relationships with members of one's own family become worse during teenage years, while relationships with other teenagers become better.

2. Parents seem to be the best target for teenagers' anger and frustrations because the parents never react violently.

3. Family ties are strained by frequent quarrels.

4. Teenagers are looking for affection. If they don't receive it from their parents, they will try to get it from their peers.

5. In some families people are often rude to one another, and the teenagers end up hurt and lonely. Some end up in trouble.

6. A strong family may be able to prevent a lot of teenage problems.

7. Relationships are better when people share the same views, the same morals, and the same principles.

8. Teenagers need confidence and attention from their parents.

9. Teenagers should not be so dependent upon their parents that they feel they can't exist without their parents.

10. Teenagers have to shift their attention from family relationships to relationships with their friends, because young people gradually move away from their homes into a wider world.

A: I agree with number 1 because . . . (it's easier to get along with people your own age/families are too emotional/the teenager's world is so different from the adult's, etc.)

B: I do, too./
I don't because . . . (I always get along great with my parents/teenagers are too young to understand each other's problems/families grow closer when you get to be a teenager.)

Ask and talk about what has already been done
Ask and talk about what has not been done yet

Steve, Diane, and John all attend the same school and sing in the school chorus. The chorus has been invited to sing in London, Paris, and Vienna during the winter vacation, with all its expenses paid. All three students are planning to go. But before they go, each of them has to do certain things. They did some of these last month, and they will do the others next month.

Look at the pictures and use them to talk with your partner about the things that Steve, Diane, and John have done already and those that they have not done yet. Then change roles.

LAST MONTH (done already)   NEXT MONTH (not done yet)

1. have passport photograph taken

LAST MONTH (done already)   NEXT MONTH (not done yet)

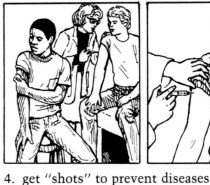 

4. get "shots" to prevent diseases

2. apply for passport

5. choose clothing to take

3. buy travelers' checks

6. decide how to get to the airport

A: Has Steve had his passport photograph taken?
B: Yes, he's already had it taken.
A: Has Diane applied for her passport?
B: No, she hasn't applied for it yet.

Language Points
Reading about leisure time activities

Nelda Wong is a friend of Carlos and Barbara and is a reporter on a newspaper in New England. Read her story and then answer the questions that follow it.

Teenagers and Their Leisure: A Special Report

by Nelda Wong, staff reporter

How do teenagers spend their leisure time? What do they do for fun? We asked a group of local high school and junior high school students these questions last week. As you might expect, sports and music are favorites with many of them, but they have lots of other interests as well. Here's what seven of these students told us they do with their leisure time.

Sheila Beattie, 15. Reads, watches TV, listens to the radio, goes shopping, goes to the movies, baby-sits, bakes food, plays soccer, talks on the phone. Does gymnastics two hours a day, five days a week. Likes ice cream and pizza. Writes letters to friends in Texas and California. Hopes to go to Stanford University in California.

Tom Leech, 14. "It's interesting to construct something and make it work." Likes basketball and baseball, says he's the ultimate TV sports fan. Enjoys dancing and parties. Likes computers. Hobby: model trains with complicated track systems. Likes little kids; baby-sits.

Bob Chang, 16. "I like solving problems, using logic and intelligence." On math team, in computer club and physics special study group. Plans to be an engineer. Hates top 10 songs and rock stations, but enjoys unusual pop songs. Likes making model airplanes.

Vanessa O'Connor, 14. Cheerleader, plays softball, jogs, runs, talks on the phone, baby-sits, sees friends, likes to shop for other people. Works on projects, writes, draws, paints, likes to read poems, dances and sings. Spends time with her family. Volunteers at a school for the handicapped. "You see how hard the kids work to overcome their problems, and you feel terrific when they succeed." Hopes to study psychology.

Tracy Kolovson, 15. Very energetic, very active in high school where she's a sophomore. Studies piano, sings in the chorus. "I love to sing and listen to music. It gives me a real lift." Loves reading, works for the school newspaper, edits the literary magazine, is in the drama club. School chairman for Students Against Drunk Driving. Does community service at Senior Citizens Center. Enjoys shopping with friends, talking on the phone, going on outings.

Susan Smith, 16. President of the Drama Club at her school—"I love acting. It's a way of really expressing your feelings." A sophmore, she writes for the school newspaper, is on the debating team. Likes reading poetry, loves basketball. Is a volunteer state capitol tour guide—"It's a chance to see how the government works and to meet people."

Matt Torino, 17. Girl-crazy and not shy about admitting it. "Oh, I have a few girlfriends. I try to talk to them two or three times a week on the phone. Then on weekends we see each other and go to the movies or watch TV." Into physical fitness, works out at the Y. Plays basketball, football, hockey. Collects baseball cards. "I collect just for fun, but in a few years some of the cards may be worth a lot of money." Plans to be an engineer.

GLOSSARY
com·pli·ca·ted—not simple; made up of many parts connected together
con·**struct**—build; put together
hand·i·capped—unable to do certain things
jog—move along faster than walking but slower than running
log·ic—correct reasoning
psy·**chol**·o·gy—the science that deals with why people think and act the way they do

With your partner, ask and answer questions about "Teenagers and Their Leisure." Also ask what else each person likes to do.

Who is the one . . .
Is Bob Chang the one . . . } who likes making model airplanes?

> A: Is Bob Chang the one who likes making model airplanes?
> B: Yes, he is.
> A: What else does he like to do?
> B: He likes to solve problems.

> A: Is Sheila Beattie the one who likes to shop for other people?
> B: No, she's the one who does gymnastics two hours a day.
> A: What else does she like to do?
> B: She likes to eat ice cream and pizza.

Writing

What do you like to do in your leisure time? Write about your leisure time activities. Use the newspaper story as a model. Before you write, talk over your ideas with your classmates or other friends. Write down as many ideas as possible, including those you get from others. Then write a first draft. Be ready to share this first draft with your partner or the class. Listen to any criticisms or suggestions they may have. Consider these criticisms and suggestions when you write your final draft. Be especially careful to correct any errors in spelling and grammar.

Reading poems—similes and metaphors

The two poems in this unit deal with the two themes of this unit: the teenage years, and relationships between people, especially between family members. Like many poems, these poems make use of *figures of speech*, expressions that use words to make comparisons in various ways. Figures of speech add vividness and help to convey an image or idea to the reader.

Two of the most frequently used figures of speech are *similes* and *metaphors*. A simile (**sim**-uh-lee) uses the words "like" or "as." (For example, "as happy as a kitten with a ball of string" or "his smile was like the sunshine.") A metaphor makes the same kind of comparison, but doesn't use "like" or "as." (For example, "a beehive of activity" or "a rainbow of colors.") Notice how simile and metaphor are used in the poem "Quarrel."

Another figure of speech that poets often use is *personification*. In personification, a thing or idea is talked about as if it were a person. Look for examples of personification in the two poems.

Read "Quarrel" and "Fifteen." Then discuss the poems with your partner or in a small group and do the activities that follow them.

FIFTEEN

by William Stafford

South of the Bridge on Seventeenth
I found back of the willows one summer
day a motorcycle with engine running
as it lay on its side, ticking over
slowly in the high grass. I was fifteen.

I admired all that pulsing gleam, the
shiny flanks, the demure headlights
fringed where it lay; I led it gently
to the road and stood with that
companion, ready and friendly. I was fifteen.

We could find the end of the road, meet
the sky on out Seventeenth. I thought about
hills, and patting the handle got back a
confident opinion. On the bridge we indulged
a forward feeling, a tremble. I was fifteen.

Thinking, back farther in the grass I found
the owner, just coming to, where he had flipped
over the rail. He had blood on his hand, was pale—
I helped him walk to his machine. He ran his hand
over it, called me good man, roared away.

I stood there, fifteen.

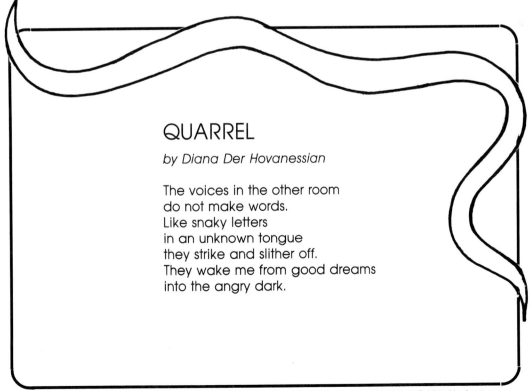

QUARREL

by Diana Der Hovanessian

The voices in the other room
do not make words.
Like snaky letters
in an unknown tongue
they strike and slither off.
They wake me from good dreams
into the angry dark.

1. **With your partner or group, decide on answers to these questions, and be ready to present your answers, together with reasons for them, to the class.**

   a. In what way are the two poems similar?
   b. How would you describe the *mood* or basic feeling of "Fifteen"? Of "Quarrel"?
   c. Why do you think the author of the longer poem chose the title "Fifteen"?
   d. What is a quarrel? Describe in your own words the experience that the author of "Quarrel" is talking about. Who do you think "the voices in the other room" belong to?
   e. How is personification used in "Fifteen"? In "Quarrel"?

2. **With your partner or group, write three examples of personification. These can be examples that you find in books or poems or examples you make up yourselves.**

Listening

1. **Before listening, read the "true-false" statements below. After listening, write on your paper *T* for true or *F* for false for each statement. The speaker is a girl of 15.**

   a. Parents believe that teenagers are capable of handling most responsibilities.
   b. Teenage boys often drift away from their fathers.
   c. The speaker is closer to her father now than she was a few years ago.
   d. The speaker is closer to her brother than to her sisters.
   e. The speaker is older than her brother.
   f. Friends don't have to like exactly the same things.
   g. Both the speaker and her best friend are interested in sports.
   h. The speaker and her best friend tell each other their secret thoughts and problems.

2. **The speaker uses the words "maturing" and "mature." Write a paragraph telling what these words mean. When does the speaker think that people mature? Do you agree? Why or why not?**

Discussion

Many television programs show family relationships or other relationships between teenagers and adults. In small groups, discuss the programs you watch. Consider the following questions. Appoint a spokesperson to report to the class on your group's discussion.

1. Do you think these programs present an accurate picture of relationships between teenagers and other age groups (adults and younger children)?
2. What kinds of families are shown on these programs? Are most American families like this? Why or why not?
3. Why do you think so many people watch and enjoy these programs?

Practice Points

1. **Read these sentences from the opening dialogue.**

    a. John, <u>who has already been on this program</u>, is a junior in high school.
    b. Teenagers <u>who don't talk to their parents</u> can wind up with some serious problems.

    The underlined parts of the two sentences (the parts beginning with <u>who</u>) are relative clauses. A relative clause gives additional information in the sentence.
    If we take the relative clause out of sentence *a*, we have taken away some information, but the basic meaning of the sentence remains the same.

    a. John, <u>who has already been on this program</u>, is a junior in high school.
    c. John is a junior in high school.

    But if we take the relative clause out of sentence *b*, the meaning of the sentence is changed. Sentence *b* is talking about a particular group of teenagers, the ones who don't talk to their parents. If the relative clause is taken out, the new sentence is talking about all teenagers, instead of a special group.

    b. Teenagers <u>who don't talk to their parents</u> can wind up with some serious problems.
    d. Teenagers can wind up with some serious problems.

    Look at sentences *e* through *n*. Some of them are like sentence *a*; that is the relative clause can be removed without changing the meaning of the sentence. Some of them are like sentence *b*; the relative clause cannot be taken out without changing the meaning.
    On your paper rewrite only the sentences that are like sentence *a*, removing the relative clause from each one.

    e. Mary, who won the school cup last year, is now a senior.
    f. Teenagers who don't study usually don't pass their exams.
    g. Parents who do not talk to their children cause serious problems.
    h. Family members who have close ties avoid misunderstandings.
    i. Parents who never react to anything are often targets for their children's anger.
    j. Teenagers, who are likely to feel unsure of themselves, need confidence, love, and understanding from their parents.
    k. Teachers who think that school work is the most important thing in the world don't always understand their students.
    l. Carlos, who is working in television now, is a good journalist.
    m. The girl who bought that record yesterday is an outstanding singer.
    n. That woman who spoke at the meeting yesterday is a friend of my parents.

2. **Write the dialogues that you practiced with your partner in the Communication Points on page 4.**

3. **Write sentences using the words in the glossary on page 5. Write a separate sentence for each word. Your sentences should be different from those in "Teenagers and Their Leisure."**

Workers are constructing a new bridge across the river.

2 A Word From Our Sponsor...

Discussion Points

Work in small groups and discuss the following questions. Appoint a spokesperson to tell the class about your group's discussion.

1. What products are most frequently advertised on TV?
2. What are your favorite commercials? Why?
3. Can you sing any songs or slogans from TV commercials? If so, which ones?
4. Does a good commercial make you buy a product? Give an example.
5. Does a bad or insulting commercial make you *not* buy a product? Give an example.
6. Have you ever bought a product because of a commercial and then decided that the commercial misled you? How can that happen?

Listening

Make a chart like this on your paper. Then listen to the three television commercials and write your answers on the chart.

	Commercial #1	Commercial #2	Commercial #3
Name of the product or service advertised.	???	???	???
Type of product or service (soap, food, etc.)	???	???	
Would the commercial make you want to buy? (yes/no)			

Skill Points

Activity 1: Different opinions

You are going to read two passages that present different opinions or points of view about the same subject. As you read them, think about the questions you discussed at the beginning of this unit.

I'M AN ADVERTISER

I'm an advertiser. You're a consumer. I'm going to communicate with you through advertising. Now advertising, as we both know, is salesmanship that takes place in the paid space and time of TV and radio commercials or newspapers and magazine ads. That's all it is. Like any salesman, its purpose is to sell. It's going to show products and services in their best light. It's not going to tell you what's good about the other guy's product or service. There are plenty of ways for you to find out about that. It's going to be corny at times; maybe there'll be too much of it now and then. We're all human.

But I promise you this. My advertising won't lie to you, and it will not deliberately try to mislead you. I won't treat you as though you were a fool or embarrass you or your family. But remember, it's a salesman. Its purpose is to persuade you to exchange your hard-earned money for my product or service.

In return for your bearing all this, I'm going to support those newspapers and magazines and radio stations and TV programs you like so much. I'm going to pay for music, situation comedies, news, stories, movies, variety shows, football games, cartoon shows, and reports on every aspect of life you may be interested in.

In the process you'll get a lot of important information to help you make choices. You'll get news about new products you like, and you'll be persuaded to try some you'll never buy again. That's the way it goes.

What do you say? Is it a deal?

DON'T BE FOOLED

It's hard to say no to television advertising. Advertisers use many tricks to get us to buy their products. They use sports figures and Hollywood celebrities to tell us how wonderful their products are. They use songwriters to write catchy songs to make us remember and buy their products. They use good-looking models to demonstrate their products. In short, they do everything possible to make their products look good and make us buy their products.

Commercials have hidden messages in them. Commercials seem to say that if you use a particular product you'll be as beautiful, intelligent, trouble-free, or happy as the actors and actresses in the commercial. They imply that only the product being advertised can bring you this happiness and peace of mind. As advertisers play the same commercial over and over again the message gradually sinks in. People eventually break down and buy the products advertised.

Often a product's performance at home is not the same as it was on television. Buyers beware: everything looks good in TV commercials. Don't be fooled. Make sure you buy products because of their quality and performance, not because of their advertising.

As you can see, the two passages present very different opinions about advertising. The first passage presents a "pro" opinion, that is, an opinion *for* advertising, *in favor of* advertising. The second one presents a "con" opinion, that is, it is *against* advertising.

People have differing opinions about many things. Look at the topics below. Choose one of them. Then write two short compositions about it. Write the first composition from a "pro" point of view, in support of the topic. Write the second composition from a "con" point of view, against the topic. Give the most convincing arguments you can for each point of view. Be prepared to read your compositions aloud to the class. Here are the topics.

a. College education should be free for everyone.
b. Husbands and wives should share housework equally.
c. The driving age should be raised to 21.
d. English should be the official language of the world.
e. People spend too much money on pets and shouldn't be allowed to keep them.

Activity 2: Interpreting a reading to find answers

The next passage is also about advertising. Read it to find answers to the questions that follow it. Remember that a TV commercial is "effective" if it makes you buy the product that is being advertised.

EFFECTIVE TV COMMERCIALS

Let's say you want to make a TV commercial. How do you begin? Long before you do any filming, you will spend a lot of time talking about and thinking about what the commercial can and should say. To get an idea of what the commercial is going to look like, you will create a storyboard.

Storyboards come in many different forms and sizes—horizontal, vertical, single pictures, etc. But most of them have three important elements: pictures that show the main action of the commercial, written descriptions of what the viewers will see, and written descriptions of what they will hear. Because television is a visual medium, there is one basic rule about storyboards. Look at the pictures first. If the pictures tell the story well, you have the makings of a good commercial.

There are several other things to be considered when making a television commercial besides a good storyboard. The first five seconds of the commercial are crucial. Tests of audience reaction show either a sharp drop or a sharp rise in interest during the first five seconds. Commercial attention does not build. Your audience can only become less interested, never more. The attention you reach in the first five seconds is the highest you will get, so don't save your punches. Offer the viewer something right at once—news, a problem to which you have the solution, a conflict that involves the viewer.

A good commercial is direct. It never makes the viewer do a lot of mental work. The basic commercial length in U.S. television is 30 seconds. The content possible in that time is outlined in the phrase: "name-claim-demonstration"—the name of your product, its benefit to the consumer, and the reason the consumer should believe it.

Too often, a viewer will remember the commercial but not the name of the brand. This is a problem particularly with new products. Showing the package on screen and saying the name is not enough. Take extra pains to stamp your product name in the viewer's mind.

People are interested in people. Your commercial will be best remembered if you show a person *on camera* with your product instead of showing only a picture and a voice-over.

Show that your product does what you said it will. At some point the housewife should admire the whiter wash, the shaver should stroke his smooth cheek, the dog should eat the dog food.

If you are lucky enough to have a product with an established brand image, your advertising must reflect that image. When you launch a new product, the very tone of your commercial tells viewers what to expect. From that moment on, it is hard to change their minds. Once you have decided on a personality for your product, keep it in every commercial.

St. Martin's Press, Inc., New York, New York. Copyright © 1976 by Kenneth Roman and Jane Maas.

Look for the simplest and most easily remembered set of words to let your consumer understand the benefit. Every word must work hard. A 30-second commercial usually allows you no more than 65 words. Be exact. Get rid of clichés and superlatives (-est/most words).

Television advertisers try to follow all of these rules in order to make the consumers buy their product. Sometimes they fail and sometimes they succeed. Only the public can be the judge of that.

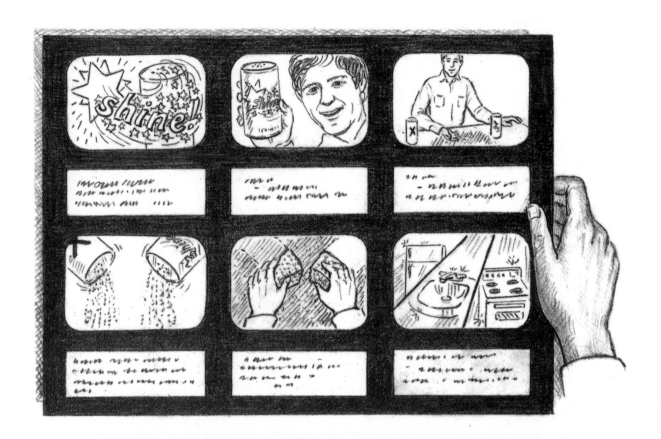

GLOSSARY

ben·e·fit—advantage, good
brand—kind, type
cli·**chés**—overused phrases
cru·cial—very important
ef·**fec**·tive—producing the correct result

hor·i·**zon**·tal—extending across from side to side
save your **punch**·es—hold back ideas, information, etc.
su·**per**·la·tives—words of high or exaggerated praise
ver·ti·cal—extending up and down

Read each statement. On your paper, tell if each of these items will make a television commercial more effective or less effective.

1. It starts out very exciting in the first 5 seconds.
2. It makes the consumer think a lot.
3. It repeats the name of the product several times so consumers will remember it.
4. It doesn't show any people.
5. The product performs well and the commercial shows it.
6. The commercial states the product's name but not its benefits.
7. The commercial has a lot of words ending in "est" or uses the word "most" very frequently.
8. The commercial is simple and uncomplicated.
9. The commercial keeps changing the personality of the product.

Activity 3: Applying standards for evaluation

Read the scripts for the following commercials. Decide if each one is good or bad according to the suggestions in "Effective TV Commercials" on pages 12 and 13. Give reasons for your decisions—for example, "It's direct," "It's too long," "It uses the right number of words," "It doesn't mention the product's name often enough." Find three or four reasons for your decision about each commercial. Write your answers on your paper.

a.

LOOPER'S BREAKFAST CEREAL

A pilot is flying an airplane making loops (circles) in the sky. He sticks his head out the cockpit window and says:

"Loopers is the crunchy cereal kids love to eat. It's tasty and sweet, and full of vitamins and minerals too. Your kids will go loopy for Loopers."

Show children eating cereal. Through trick photography, have kids spin around in a complete circle after eating a spoonful of Loopers. Return to pilot.

"Buy Loopers breakfast cereal at your local supermarket. Loopers is delicious for breakfast and good for snacks too."

Pilot does one more loop and then lands in a supermarket parking lot. Window of supermarket is filled with Loopers cereal.

b.

STACY'S RESTAURANT

A man is standing in front of a restaurant. He is pointing to it. He says:

"This is my restaurant. I've worked here for many years. My father started this restaurant but he's retired now. He lives in Miami. We serve great food here. Come down and try it sometime. We have chicken, mashed potatoes. Mmmmm. They melt in your mouth. Roast beef, corn. All your favorites. Our chef, Vincent, is one of the best cooks in the entire world. His chili is famous from coast-to-coast. Come down to my restaurant soon. I'll look forward to seeing you."

c.

OWL BROOK BOTTLED WATER

A very rich and sophisticated woman is sitting in an expensive restaurant. Other diners watch as 5 waiters, each carrying a tray with a drink on it, approach her. She speaks angrily to the first 4, dismissing each one in turn with a wave of her hand.

"Coffee? Too much caffeine.
Iced Tea? Never!
Soda? Too many calories.
Diet Soda? I hate the aftertaste."

As the 5th waiter approaches, the woman's angry face turns to a delighted smile. The waiter is carrying a tray with a bottle of Owl Brook water. The woman says:

"Owl Brook, of course."

The waiter pours the water into an ice-filled glass while an announcer says,

"Owl Brook, the perfect drink straight from nature to satisfy your thirst. Natural mineral water from our pure, bubbling brook. Owl Brook, the thirst quencher for wise drinkers."

d.

SPLASH LAUNDRY DETERGENT

A woman stands on a high diving board. She makes a perfect dive into an Olympic swimming pool. The crowd around the pool cheers. When she comes to the surface, the woman says:

"Sure, I like to make a splash at the pool, but I like to make a splash at home, too."

Scene changes to woman at home taking clothes out of washing machine.

"That's why I use Splash laundry detergent. It cleans my family's clothes beautifully. A dash of Splash brightens colors and whitens whites. Make a splash in your home, too, with Splash detergent. You'll get clean clothes in a flash with Splash."

e.

POPLIN'S TOOTHPASTE

A tube of toothpaste is sitting on a table. Next to it is a glass of water and a red toothbrush. An announcer's voice says:

"People must brush their teeth three times a day, after their morning, afternoon, and evening meals. There's no excuse for not brushing. It's a bad habit not to brush. You can get cavities or bad breath. When you brush, you should use Poplin's toothpaste. It will make your teeth look white as snow and your breath smell as sweet as roses. There's no other toothpaste in the supermarket that's as good as Poplin's toothpaste. You should buy it."

Activity 4: Applying standards in writing

Now use the rules for effective commercials to write your own commercial. Make it interesting and persuasive: make your viewers want to rush right out and buy the product. Write your commercial about one of the following products—or make up a product or service of your own.

a new sports car	paper towels	a new soft drink
new chocolate chip cookies	perfume	bread
dishwashing liquid	canned soup	dog food

Literary Points

Activity 1: Similes and metaphors

Advertisers like to use words that will create pictures in the viewers' minds as well as on the screen. So they often tell you that their product is like something that people already know and like. To do this, they use similes and metaphors. As you have learned, a *simile* compares two things using "like" or "as." A *metaphor* makes a comparison without using "like" or "as."

Write a simile or metaphor for each of the following products. Be sure to give the product a name. Look at the example.

house paint

For a house as fresh as spring use Brown's paints!
Use the paints that are like the rainbow!
Brown's paints—the rainbow in a can of paint!

a. a fast car	c. a bleach that gets clothes very white	e. French bread
b. a sweet candy	d. a nice-smelling hand soap	f. perfume

Activity 2: Reading a poem

Long before television was invented, poets were using similes and metaphors to help convey feelings and moods. Poets still use similes and metaphors. Eve Merriam's poem about poetry, " 'I,' Says the Poem," is a good example. Read the poem and find three similes and three metaphors. With a partner or a small group, discuss these similes and metaphors and tell why you think the poet chose them and what she was trying to tell her readers. Then look at the last three lines of the poem. How do they fit in with your discussion? What do they tell you about reading a poem? How are they a metaphor in themselves?

"I," SAYS THE POEM

by Eve Merriam

"I," says the poem arrogantly,
"I am a cloud,
I am a tree.

I am a city,
I am the sea,
I am a golden
Mystery."

How can it be?

A poem is written
by some someone,
someone like you,
or someone like me

who blows his nose,
who breaks shoelaces,
who hates and loves,
who loses gloves,
who eats, who weeps,
who laughs, who sleeps,

an ordinary he or she
extraordinary as you or me

whose thoughts stretch high
as clouds in the sky,

whose memories
root deep as trees,

whose feelings choke
like city smoke,

whose fears and joys in waves redound
like the ocean's tidal sound,

who daily solves a mystery:
each hour is new, what will it be?

"I," says the poem matter-of-factly,
"I am a cloud,
I am a tree.

I am a city,
I am the sea,

I am a golden
Mystery."

But adds the poem silently,
I cannot speak until you come.
Reader, come, come with me.

From IT DOESN'T ALWAYS HAVE TO RHYME by Eve Merriam. Copyright © 1964 by Eve Merriam. Reprinted by permission of Marian Reiner for the author.

CARLOS: This is Studio 1, where we broadcast the news.

BARBARA: Of course! I've seen it on the screen at home! What's going on? Are they going to do a news broadcast?

CARLOS: Not right now. The news isn't on until six o'clock. This is a special weather bulletin about the hurricane.

BARBARA: Is it going to hit here?

CARLOS: It looks that way, Barbara. It might hit tonight. The hurricane watch has been changed to a hurricane warning. Look! They're ready to go on the air.

BARBARA: Shouldn't we leave the studio?

CARLOS: No, we don't need to. But we'd better move, in case they want to use this camera.

JOEL: Good afternoon. This is Joel Matthews, your Channel 8 meteorologist, with a special bulletin on Hurricane Flora. The National Hurricane Center has just informed us that Flora has turned inland and is moving toward the southern New York–New England coast. The hurricane watch has been changed to a hurricane warning from Sandy Hook, New Jersey, to Cape Cod, Massachusetts. Tides up to 15 feet are expected, and low-lying coastal areas should be evacuated as early as possible before escape routes are closed. Heavy rain with local amounts of 8 to 10 inches is expected here in the city and on Long Island, southern Connecticut, and Rhode Island.

We don't know yet just where Flora will come ashore, but we'll keep you posted. Stay tuned to Channel 8 for the latest news on Hurricane Flora. We now return you to our regular programming.

Communication Points
Give advice and explanations

1. **Read the directions that the National Hurricane Center gives to protect people who live near the coast of the United States. Then read the explanations. Match each of the directions with its explanation. On your paper write the directions and explanations, joining them with one of these linking words or expressions: *so that, in case, because*.**

Watch the news from June through November so that you can see if there are any signs of hurricanes.

**NATIONAL HURRICANE CENTER DIRECTIONS
TO FOLLOW IN CASE OF HURRICANES**

a. Watch the news from June through November.
b. Store fresh drinking water in jugs and stock up on canned food.
c. Get the car ready to go.
d. Make sure that you know all the roads that lead inland.
e. Don't stay at home if you live near water.
f. Make sure the batteries of your radio are not dead.
g. Keep listening to the radio.
h. Don't stay near the windows.
i. Don't leave valuable items on the ground floor of your house.

EXPLANATIONS

  j. You may have to spend several days without electricity.
  k. The main roads may be jammed with traffic.
  l. You may have to leave in a hurry.
m. Water may flood the lower floors.
  n. You can hear weather reports even if the electricity is off.
  o. They might break during the hurricane.
  p. You can have continuous information about the hurricane.
  q. You can see if there are any signs of hurricanes.
  r. You house could be washed away by the waves.

2. **Ask and answer with your partner.**

> A: Why should I watch the news from June through November?
> B: So that you can see if there are any signs of hurricanes.

> A: Why should I get the car ready to go?
> B: In case you have to leave in a hurry.

Make predictions

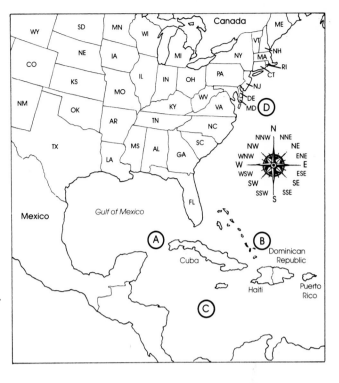

Look at the map of the eastern part of the United States. The letter A shows the position of a hurricane. Here are some facts about it.

Hurricane name: Archie
Tides: 12 feet
Rain: 9–11 inches
Wind speed: 140 miles per hour
Hurricane direction: north northwest (NNW)
Hurricane speed: 18 miles an hour.

1. **Decide where you think Archie will come ashore and write a special hurricane warning bulletin based on the facts above. Use Joel's bulletin on page 17 as a model. Notice that Joel uses the passive form of some verbs.**

   The hurricane watch has been changed . . . .
   Tides up to 15 feet are expected . . . .
   . . . escape routes are closed.

   Use the passive form of verbs in your bulletin wherever you can. Write your bulletin on your paper.

2. **Now talk with your partner about the bulletin.**

   > A: What kind of tides are expected?
   > B: We expect tides up to 12 feet.

3. **The letters B, C, and D on the map show where other hurricanes are. On your paper, write a fact list for one of these. Choose your facts from this list.**

Tides	Rain	Wind speed	Direction	Speed of travel
9 feet	7 inches	100 miles per hour	north	10 miles per hour
10 feet	to	to	north northwest	to
11 feet	17 inches	200 miles per hour	northwest	22 miles per hour
13 feet			north northeast	
15 feet			northeast	

   Give your hurricane a name (man's or woman's) starting with the letter of the hurricane on the map (B, C, or D). Then answer your partner's questions about it, and ask him or her where the hurricane will come ashore. Then change roles.

   > A: How much rain is expected?
   > B: We expect 7 to 9 inches of rain.
   > A: What's the wind speed?
   > B: It's about 180 miles per hour.

   > B: Where do you think Hurricane . . . will come ashore?
   > A: It will probably come ashore at . . . .
   > B: When is it expected to get there?
   > A: It'll probably get there in about . . . hours.

Language Points
Reading about history
CAMILLE

Satellite photo of hurricane Camille

The storm wasn't spectacular when it was born on August 5, 1969. On satellite pictures it appeared merely as a cloud patch moving west from Africa. It wasn't a hurricane yet. A storm must have winds of at least 74 miles per hour to earn that name.

As the storm approached the United States, the National Hurricane Center in Miami, Florida, sent up airplanes to study it. On August 15, the storm's winds were measured at over 100 miles per hour. It was named "Hurricane Camille."

On the evening of August 15, Camille slammed into Cuba. It battered that island with high winds and ten inches of rain. When Camille was through with Cuba, three people were dead. The hurricane then headed for the southern coast of the United States.

Over the warm waters of the Gulf of Mexico Camille grew stronger than ever. On August 16, hurricane hunters who flew into Camille clocked its winds at 160 miles per hour. That day the National Hurricane Center called for a hurricane watch extending along the coast from St. Marks, Florida, to Biloxi, Mississippi. The hurricane watch meant that coastal residents should prepare for the possibility of the storm striking land within two days. Later on August 16 the hurricane watch was changed to a hurricane warning. The warning meant that the hurricane was expected to strike a specific place within the next twelve hours.

On Sunday, August 17, an airplane flying inside Camille clocked its winds at more than 200 miles per hour. Those tremendous winds—plus huge waves—were expected to smash the Mississippi shore by evening. Throughout the afternoon, thousands of people left their beachfront homes and went inland. Police and Civil Defense officials traveled along the Mississippi coastline advising those remaining to leave. Most people left their beachfront homes, but some refused to. By evening, 100,000 persons along the Gulf Coast had left their homes.

Those who remained had no idea that they were about to be struck by one of the mightiest hurricanes in United States history.

Camille first touched the Mississippi coast at about nine in the evening. "The wind was the worst noise I have ever heard in my life," remembered Richard I. Hadden, an attorney who lived in Pass Christian, Mississippi. "It sounded like a thousand freight trains and a thousand airplanes coming right at you."

The tremendous winds tore off roofs, ripped out buildings, and hurled cars through the air. They were among the strongest ever measured in a hurricane. And they blew hour after hour. But the winds weren't the greatest killer in Camille. They created tremendous walls of water on the Gulf of Mexico. Ten to fifteen-foot waves crashed into the coastal cities. Buildings were washed right off their foundations. As the buildings were ripped apart, the people inside were thrown into the swirling water.

Throughout the night, people floating on wreckage fought for their lives. Then, before dawn, the wind lessened, and the water began its return to the Gulf of Mexico.

Mississippi's Gulf Coast looked as if it had been hit by a huge bomb. Bodies, bricks, trees, furniture, and railroad tracks lay strewn about. Many things could be seen where they didn't belong. In Biloxi, a shrimp boat was perched on some railroad tracks. In Gulfport a boat that had been carried several blocks inland sat in front of the First Baptist Church.

Living animals wandered about, dazed. At Pascagoula, Mississippi, thousand of water moccasins invaded the town. These poisonous snakes had been driven out of the flooded rivers and marshes. An alligator that had been driven from a Louisiana bayou was seen wandering about in the town of Bay St. Louis, Mississippi.

Once a hurricane reaches land, it weakens. Most experts thought that after Camille battered the Mississippi coast its killing days were over. As Camille churned northeastward, its winds did lessen. But the hurricane's clouds still carried tons of water. On the night of August 19–20, tremendous rainstorms assaulted Virginia and West Virginia. Up to a foot of water fell in places. The water caused rivers to flood, washed away bridges and houses, and created mud slides. Most people were sleeping. They had no warning. More than 100 died in these floods, raising Camille's United States death toll to 324.

On August 20, Hurricane Camille returned to the ocean where it had been born. Its winds

dropped to 65 miles per hour and then less. Off the coast of Newfoundland, Camille disappeared. But those who had experienced her howling winds and raging waters would never forget her.

GLOSSARY

bat·ter—to strike or hit very hard, with tremendous force

clocked—made a record of speed or time

howl·ing—making a loud, mournful sound

huge—very large

might·i·est—strongest

strewn a·**bout**—thrown or dropped in several places

weak·ened—got less strong

---

1. **Read "Camille." Then copy or trace a simple map of the eastern half of the United States. Put dates and places on your map to locate the path of Camille from the time it came near the coast. Then ask and answer questions about Camille with your partner.**

    > A: Where was Camille on August 15?
    > B: It was in Cuba.

2. **Discuss these questions with your partner or a group of classmates. Finally, write your answers to the questions.**

    a. There are many hurricanes each year in the United States. Why do you think the authors chose this one to write about?

    b. Why do you think the National Hurricane Center sends out two kinds of messages about hurricanes, the "Hurricane Watch" and the "Hurricane Warning?" What is the main difference between these two warnings?

    c. How does the National Hurricane Center measure the strength of a hurricane? Would you like to be one of the people who does this? Why or why not?

    d. Why do you think the National Hurricane Center is located in Miami, Florida?

    e. What effects of Hurricane Camille caused the greatest losses? Could any of these losses have been prevented, and if so, how?

Reading about science
WHAT IS A HURRICANE?

Many of the hurricanes that strike the United States begin as storms off the west coast of Africa. They churn slowly westward until they strike the West Indies and the southeastern coast of the United States. Once over land, the hurricanes usually weaken and then disappear.

The United States isn't the only place that gets battered by these fierce storms. But in other parts of the world they may have different names. In the North Pacific Ocean, for example, they are called typhoons. In the Indian Ocean and the South Pacific, they are usually called tropical cyclones.

It is not known for sure how a hurricane begins. According to the theory accepted by most scientists, it all starts when the heat of the sun warms some ocean water. The surface of the water evaporates, forming a cloud of warm, wet air that moves upward. As this warm air rises, other air rushes in to replace it. This air is also heated and moistened by the warm ocean surface. It begins to rise and form clouds, heating the air around it. Eventually, a large mass of warm, moist air with rain clouds is formed over the ocean. The clouds contain huge amounts of water.

Because the air is warm, it expands. It becomes less dense and lighter, and forms an area of low pressure. More air near the ocean surface now rushes in. However, this air doesn't just flow straight in. It spirals in, like water going down a bathtub drain. (This spiraling, or spinning motion, is caused by the rotation, or turning, of the earth, both in the hurricane and in the bathtub.) The air

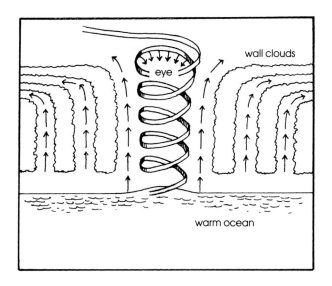

goes faster and faster as it spirals inward. It rises. Soon it has formed an "eye" or center, about 20 miles wide, surrounded by spinning "wall clouds." The winds in the wall clouds can reach a speed of 200 miles an hour or even more, and the storm can be several hundred miles wide.

The whole storm is now spinning like a top. It is carried across the warm ocean by the wind at a speed of, usually, 15 to 20 miles an hour.

Finally the storm moves over land or cold water. Without its "fuel force" (the warm ocean), its winds begin to grow less powerful. Eventually it dies, but often not before leaving a path of destruction in its wake.

1. **Put these sentences in the correct sequence. Then write a paragraph on your paper using these sentences, to describe how a hurricane is formed.**

   a. The whole storm is carried across the warm ocean.
   b. The air that moves in to replace the rising air spirals faster and faster and continues to rise.
   c. As the wet warm air rises and expands, air moves in to replace it.
   d. In the beginning the ocean water is heated by the sun.
   e. A large mass of warm, moist air expands as it rises.
   f. A cloud of warm air begins to rise.
   g. When the storm finally moves across land or cold water it becomes weaker and dies.
   h. Now the storm can spiral as fast as 200 miles an hour.

2. **With your partner, match each of the words below with its meaning. If you're not sure, find the words in the Dialogue (page 17), "Camille," (pages 20–21), or "What Is a Hurricane?" (page 22).**

a. evacuate
b. flood
c. hurricane
d. hurricane hunter
e. hurricane warning
f. hurricane watch
g. rotate
h. storm
i. spiral motion
j. tide
k. tropical cyclone
l. typhoon

m. to turn around a fixed point
n. the regular rise and fall of ocean water twice each day
o. a rough weather condition with wind, rain, and often lightning
p. a message from a local weather office saying that a hurricane is expected to strike a specific place within the next 12 hours
q. water that overflows and covers land that is normally dry
r. an airplane pilot who flies into a hurricane to study it
s. to leave a threatened area
t. a message from a local weather office saying that a hurricane is expected to strike an area within two days
u. a huge, powerful windstorm that whirls in a circular motion
v. a hurricane that occurs in the Indian Ocean or the South Pacific
w. a spinning motion toward the center and up or down
x. a hurricane that occurs in the North Pacific Ocean

Writing

Write a bulletin for a hurricane warning on television or radio like the one in the dialogue (page 17). Use the following information.

Speed of wind: 145 miles per hour
Amount of rain: 10½ inches
High tides: 18 feet
Storm location: 200 mi. west of Havana, Cuba

Direction of storm: north
Where storm will hit coast: between Houston, TX, and New Orleans, LA

Listening

Listen to Carlos interviewing a meteorologist and answer these questions on your paper.

1. Where does the word *hurricane* come from?
2. Who were the sailors that lost their lives because of hurricanes in the 16th and 17th centuries?
3. How far from Galveston harbor was a ship found after a terrible hurricane?
4. How long could the United States be furnished with electricity by the power generated by a hurricane?
5. What creatures were found in New England after a hurricane?
6. How many people died in what is considered the deadliest hurricane that has ever hit our planet?

Practice Points

1. **On your paper, match each sentence in column A with a sentence in column B and join the sentences with *so that, in case,* or *because*. (These words are called *linking words* because they link together or join two different ideas.) Use each sentence only once.**

I'll turn on the radio.   I can hear about the hurricane.

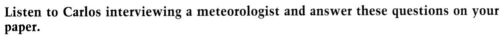

I'll turn on the radio so that I can hear about the hurricane.

A

a. I'm going to get up early Sunday morning.
b. These days I spend more time studying.
c. Janelle is taking her umbrella to work.
d. I gave the cat lots of food this morning.
e. We left a light on in the house.
f. Joanne didn't send the store a check.
g. I'm buying lots of food while the sun's out.

B

h. No one knew we weren't at home.
i. The snow is very heavy this week.
j. My grades were't very good last semester.
k. I can watch the sun rise.
l. The amount on the bill was wrong.
m. I'm not going to be home until late.
n. It starts to rain early.

2. There are two ways to give instructions. Read the instructions that go with these pictures.

All windows and doors should be closed tight.

Fresh water should be stored in jugs.

Radio batteries should be replaced.

These instructions emphasize things: window, doors, water, batteries. They use the *passive* forms of the verbs *close, store, replace.* When you use the passive form of a verb you always use the verb *to be.* The same instructions can be written in a different way.

Close all windows and doors tight.

Store fresh water in jugs.

Replace radio batteries.

These instructions emphasize the action that is done and the person who is going to do it. They use the *active* forms of the verbs.

3. Look at the instructions below. With your partner, change each one to the active form.

a. The receiver is lifted.

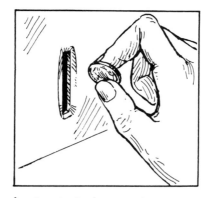

b. A coin is deposited.

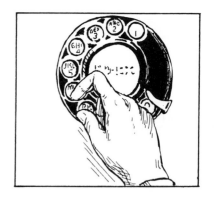

c. The number is dialed.

A: The receiver is lifted.
B: Lift the receiver.

4. Now look at these statements.

Weather forecasts are broadcast by Channel 8 every hour.

Floods are often caused by hurricanes.

Great damage can be done by high winds.

These statements emphasize what is done and not what or who does it. They use the passive forms of the verbs *broadcast, cause, do.* The same statements can be written in a different way.

Channel 8 broadcasts weather forecasts every hour.

Hurricanes often cause floods.

High winds can do great damage.

These statements emphasize the "doers": Channel 8, hurricanes, high winds. They use the active forms of the verbs.

5. Now look at the following pictures and statements. The statements use the passive forms of the verbs. With your partner, change them to statements using the active forms.

a. The meat is sliced by the butcher.

b. The football is thrown by the quarterback.

c. Chopsticks are used by Japanese diners.

d. The car is washed by Bill.

e. Every night the front door is locked by Janet.

f. The hot dogs were cooked by Federico last night.

A: The meat is sliced by the butcher.
B: The butcher slices the meat.

6. **Look at these pictures and statements. They all use the active forms of the verbs. With your partner, change them to statements using the passive forms.**

a. Josefina hammered in the last nail.

b. Max made the salad for dinner.

c. Jim painted the room in one day.

d. Yoshiko made the posters for the Fourth of July picnic.

e. Jose paid the electric bill last week.

f. Natasha drove Mrs. Wong to the hospital last Friday.

A: Josefina hammered in the last nail.
B: The last nail was hammered in by Josefina.

The American Cowhand 4

Discussion Points

**Work in small groups and discuss the following questions. Appoint a spokesperson
to tell the class about your group's discussion.**

1. What two small words make up the word *cowhand*? Each of these words stands for more
   than the exact meaning of the word. What does each of them stand for? What other word is
   used instead of *cowhand*? Why is it a less accurate word?
2. What did cowhands do 100 years ago? What do they do now?
3. This unit is called "The American Cowhand." In what other parts of the world do you think
   there might be cowhands?

 Listening

Listen to Carlos interviewing four people on a program about cowhands. Take notes on your paper on the following facts.

1. the period when cowhands became important for the cattle industry
2. the kind of people who were inspired by the cowhands and their life
3. the daily distance covered in a trail drive
4. the number of cowhands involved in a large "roundup"
5. the means of transportation used by modern cowhands

Skill Points

Activity 1: Reading for details

Read the newspaper story to find the following facts. Write the answers on your paper.

a. Manuel Pedrillo

a. name of rodeo winner
b. where the winner is from
c. where the rodeo took place
d. amount the winner has earned so far
e. height of the winner
f. weight of the winner

g. what the winner did with John Silver
h. the special prize the winner received
i. amount he won at Red Lodge
j. where he practiced roping as a child
k. the person who taught him how to use the rope
l. amount won last year as PRCA champion

Champion Cowboy Wins Again

Cowboy champion Manuel ("Manolo") Pedrillo from Palo Alto, California, was the top winner yesterday in the Fourth of July rodeo in St. Paul, Oregon. He has already earned $8780, the largest amount of money won by anyone in the eleven professional rodeos held so far this year and was professional cowboy champion last year.

Pedrillo, a California cowboy who is 5'7" tall and weighs 160 pounds, won his first $820 in May when he wrapped up a calf in 11 seconds. Team roping, Pedrillo's speciality, was next in the rodeo in May. He and John Silver of Canby, Oregon, took 7.3 seconds to rope a calf, and they each won another $513. For this double win, Pedrillo was awarded a special prize, a silver belt buckle for the all-around cowboy. In

June Pedrillo went to the Red Lodge rodeo and won another $650.

As a member of the Professional Rodeo Cowboys Association (PRCA), he toured the states performing in the biggest rodeos and winning left and right. And the rodeo season isn't over yet!

Pedrillo started his rodeo career practicing with a rope in his parents' living room. His grandfather worked with him and taught him how to use the rope properly. For nearly a decade Manolo and his brother Jerry have dominated all the major roping rodeos. Last year Pedrillo was the top money-maker among the professional cowboys, and won the PRCA championship with more than $30,000 in earnings.

GLOSSARY
earn·ings—salary, money paid for work
prop·erly—correctly
toured—traveled
win·ning left and right—winning constantly, at every location

Activity 2: Scanning for specific facts

The next passage is a different kind of reading but the subject is the same. Scan it quickly to find answers to these questions. (As you know, to *scan* is to look rapidly through a written passage to find a particular fact or facts.) Write your answers on your paper.

a. Who was the first person who brought cattle to America?
b. Where did Coronado bring cattle?
c. When did Cortés bring horses to Mexico?
d. What was the period of great expansion in cattle ranching in America?
e. In what period did cowhands' work change?

COWHAND–HORSE–CATTLE

When most people think of cowhands they think of the West in the 1860s. The story of cowhand-horse-cattle is much older than that, however. It dates back to Christopher Columbus's second voyage to the New World. It was Columbus who brought the first cows—or cattle—to the Americas in the 1490s. The Spanish explorer Francisco Coronado brought cattle into Mexico several years later.

In 1519, Hernando Cortés, another Spanish explorer, brought the first domesticated horses into Mexico. There had been wild horses in the Americas in prehistoric times, but they had all died off thousands of years ago. Many of the horses brought into Mexico escaped to the North. Their descendants ran freely in herds and were called mustangs.

The first herd of cattle to come to Texas was from Mexico. It was a small herd of only 200. But there was a growing demand for beef in the northern and eastern states. Texas was an ideal place to raise cattle to meet that demand. More herds were brought in. The cattle began to multiply, and by the 1860s, the American cowhand entered the picture of "cowhand-horse-cattle." The cowhands were needed to round up, or gather together, the cattle from the open plains and drive them in large herds to the "cowtowns" up north. These were the towns where the railroads from the East ended. At the cowtowns, the cattle were loaded on trains for the trip East.

The profits from cattle ranching were great. Between 1860 and 1880 many people came West to engage in cattle raising. There were Europeans, Easterners, and Southerners. Thousands of black Americans, freed in 1865 after the American Civil War, became cowhands as well. For 20 years cowhands drove cattle up from Texas to one of the cowtowns, the great railroad cities of Abilene, Kansas; Kansas City, Missouri; or Cheyenne, Wyoming.

The cattle drives ended when the railroads expanded. In addition, homesteaders started to use the open range, the land where the cattle grazed, for farming. The homesteaders put up barbed wire fences around their land to prevent the free movement of cattle. It was the end of the open range and the cattle drives.

After the 1880s there were very few cattle drives, and little use of the old cattle trails. Cowhands returned to the ranches. They still herded cattle, but they also dug postholes, fixed fences, repaired windmills, drove mowers, and baled hay. The days of the long cattle drives were gone forever.

GLOSSARY	
barbed—pointed, sharp	herd—group of cattle
beef—meat from cattle	i•de•al—perfect
ex•pand•ed—got larger	plains—flat, grassy land
graze—feed upon grass	

Activity 3: Sequencing

On your paper, write the following events in the correct sequence, or chronological order. (*Chronological order* tells how events happened according to their dates or times.)

a. Cortés brings horses into Mexico.
b. Homesteaders close off the open range.
c. The first herd of cattle is brought into Texas.
d. The American Civil War ends.
e. Columbus brings cattle into the New World.

Activity 4: Interpreting a reading to find answers

Read the passage again and decide if each of the following sentences is true or false. On your paper write the number of the sentence and the letter *T* for true or *F* for false. If the sentence is false, rewrite the entire sentence, changing it to make it true.

The story of cowhand-horse-cattle dates back to the 1860s.

F. The story of cowhand-horse-cattle dates back to the 1490s.

a. Columbus brought cattle, horses, and sheep on his second voyage to the Americas.
b. Coronado brought cattle into Mexico.
c. Wild cows running freely in herds are called mustangs.
d. Two thousand cattle were in the first herd brought into Texas.
e. In the 1860s cowhands were needed to round up the cattle and drive them over the trails.
f. Cowhands drove the cattle south to the railroads.
g. Europeans, Easterners, and Southerners were some of the groups who joined the cattle boom.
h. Abilene, Cheyenne, and Kansas City were the great homesteader towns.
i. After the 1890s the main job of the cowhands was long trail drives.

Activity 5: Vocabulary check

Each of the words or word pairs in the box is used in the story "Cowhand-Horse-Cattle." Reread the story and find a meaning for each of the words from the definitions below. Then write the word and the definition on your paper.

barbed wire - c. a sharp pointed material used to make fences.

barbed wire	to bale	mustang	ranch
cattle drive	to herd	open range	round up

a. a kind of farm where beef cattle are raised
b. a wild horse
c. a sharp, pointed material used to make fences
d. a group of animals
e. to tie up in a large bundle
f. to push and guide a large group of cattle
g. bringing together of a scattered group of cattle
h. a wide unfenced area of land over which cattle roam freely

Activity 6: Cowboy trails

**When cowhands drove cattle to the "cowtowns," they followed one of several
different trails. The map shows four of these cattle trails, the Chisholm Trail, the
Western Trail, the Northern Trail, and the Goodnight-Loving Trail. Use the map
to answer the following questions on your paper.**

a. Each of the trails began in Texas. Tell where (near what city or cities) each of the four
   trails ended.
b. Which trail went farthest east?
c. Which trail went farthest west?
d. Which trail passed through the famous cowboy town of Dodge City, Kansas?

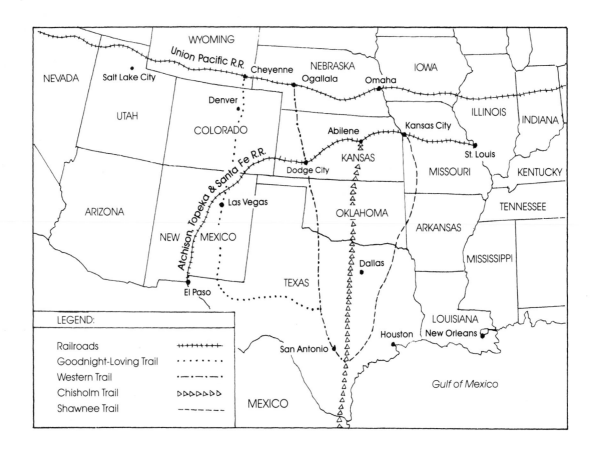

Activity 7: Writing

**Many people left Europe and the eastern part of the United States to go west and
become cowhands during the 1860s. Imagine that you are one of these
adventurers. Write a letter to the people you are leaving behind—family, friends,
girlfriend, or boyfriend. Explain where you are going, what you will be doing
there, and why you have decided to go there. Then write a second letter telling
what your life on the trail is like.**

    **Before writing, talk the assignment over with your classmates or friends. Write
down as many ideas as possible, including ideas and information you get from
others. Then write a first draft. Share this draft with your partner, a small group,
or the class. Listen to their criticisms and suggestions. Use these criticisms and
suggestions as you prepare your final draft. Be careful to include any corrections
in spelling and grammar, and use your best handwriting.**

Literary Points

Activity 1: Rhyme

When words have the same ending sound, we say that they *rhyme*. Some examples of rhyming words are *brown* and *town*, *sell* and *tell*, and *making* and *taking*. Rhyme is often used in poems, songs, and folklore.

Look at the examples below. Copy each example on your paper and complete it by filling in the blank with a rhyming word.

In October the leaves are BROWN
On every tree in the . . . .

*In October the leaves are brown
On every tree in the town.*

a. When the cat's AWAY,
   the mice will . . . .

b. There was ease in Casey's bearing as he
   stepped into his PLACE.
   There was pride in Casey's bearing and a
   smile on Casey's . . . .

c. Early to bed and early to RISE
   Makes a man healthy, wealthy, and . . . .

d. Better be early and have to WAIT
   Than go too slow and come too . . . .

e. I cannot tell how the truth may BE;
   I say the tale as 'twas said to . . . .

Activity 2: Onomatopoeia

Some words sound like the things or actions they describe. The word *onomatopoeia* (on-uh-mat-uh-pē-uh) is used to describe these words. Think of *bang, crash, crunch,* and *whisper.* Writers often use these words to help their readers ''hear'' in their minds the things the writers are describing. When Samuel Taylor Coleridge, an English poet, wanted to describe the ice that surrounded a ship he wrote, ''It cracked and growled and roared and howled . . . .'' As we hear these words, we can almost hear the chunks of ice being blown against each other and against the ship.

   Animal sounds are a good example of onomatopoeia. In English we say cats *meow*. Meow sounds like the cry of a cat. We call the sound of a cow *moo*, because that is exactly what it sounds like.

Match the 2 columns below. Find the correct sound in column B which describes the object named in column A. Write the answers on your paper.

A	B
a. the ocean waves	i. twittered
b. the busy bees	j. boomed
c. the escaping gas	k. screeched
d. the happy canaries	l. buzzed
e. dynamite	m. sizzled
f. the cooking bacon	n. splashed
g. the frightened mouse	o. hissed
h. car brakes	p. squeaked

JEAN: Hi, Carlos. How's the documentary coming? Got any more ideas for it?

CARLOS: I think so. Remember my girlfriend, Barbara? Well, she told me yesterday that there was a psychologist out in California who had taught a gorilla named Koko to talk, using sign language.

JEAN: Sounds interesting.

CARLOS: It sure does. The psychologist is Dr. Francine Patterson, and she lives near San Francisco. She's written a couple of books.

JEAN: Are they about the gorilla?

CARLOS: That's right. Barbara got one of the books for her young niece. She said it told about Koko's pet kitten, and that it had pictures of Koko, the kitten, and Dr. Patterson in it. I'm going to see if we can get any movies or videotapes of Koko and the kitten.

JEAN: Does Koko still have the kitten?

CARLOS: The book said that she had a different kitten now. The first one was killed by an automobile.

JEAN: That must have been hard on Koko. Well, it sounds like a good possibility for a program.

CARLOS: That's what I thought. I'll keep you posted on what I find out.

JEAN: You do that. See you, Carlos!

Communication Points
Report what people say

1. Carlos asked Barbara a number of questions about Dr. Patterson and Koko. Then he told Jean about his conversation with Barbara.

Here are some of the things Barbara told Carlos.

Here is the way Carlos reported Barbara's words. Notice how the verbs change in his reported speech.

Dr. Patterson's a developmental psychologist with a degree from Stanford University.

Barbara told me that Dr. Patterson was a developmental psychologist with a degree from Stanford University.

She lives in Woodside, California.

She said that Dr. Patterson lived in Woodside, California.

Koko uses sign language to communicate.

The book said that Koko used sign language.

Koko knows about 500 words. She uses more than 100 different words every day.

It also said that Koko knew about 500 words and used more than 100 different ones every day.

Koko can communicate how she feels and what she wants.

It said that Koko could communicate how she felt and what she wanted.

The book shows how Koko expresses love, anger, sorrow, and joy.

It showed how she expressed love, anger, sorrow, and joy.

2. With your partner, ask and answer about what each of these people said. Then change roles.

1. Joe Doyle

2. Kathy Bloom

3. Larry Smith

4. Alvaro Martinez

A: What did Joe Doyle say?
B: He said he planned to run for Congress next year.

Report people's questions

Ask and answer with your partner.

A: What did the woman ask the Martian?
B: She asked him who he was.

Ask and answer with your partner. Use *if*.

A: What did one woman ask the other?
B: She asked her if she lived there.

Language Points

Reading about science
KANZI

Several years ago a four-year-old chimpanzee at a center near Atlanta, Georgia, learned to communicate in a way no other animals had ever attained. The chimpanzee, named Kanzi, communicated with people by using symbols on a keyboard. Scientists said that Kanzi was the first ape to show a wide understanding of spoken English words.

Interest in "talking" apes first arose some fifteen years earlier when Washoe, raised as a human child, learned to make hand signs for many words. Apes must use hand signs or other symbols because they are not able to pronounce consonants.

When he was young, Kanzi played in the laboratory while scientists taught symbols to his mother. When Kanzi was two and a half, the scientists realized with amazement that he was able to match symbols with objects. They decided to see if Kanzi could learn language the way a human child does. But because Kanzi was an ape, not a human child, they tried to create a world that was half human and half more natural for an ape.

Kanzi had great freedom to go about the grounds of the center. He used a keyboard to say where he wanted to go, what he wanted to eat, and what games he wanted to play. Two people accompanied Kanzi and his half-sister, Mulika, from morning to night. Six other persons provided the young animals with a "family."

Kanzi and Mulika started a typical day at 7:30 in the morning by watching television. On a special program made just for them, they saw objects together with the symbols that stood for them. Sometimes a giant rabbit appeared on the TV, talking about new things, while symbols were shown in the corner of the screen. The same giant rabbit also appeared now and then off TV. The scientists worked hard to make sure that Kanzi did not discover **that** it was really one of his teachers in costume.

By 9:00 A.M., Kanzi and Mulika were playing games outside the laboratory. Tag was a favorite game. Sometimes Kanzi would tell one teacher to chase the other while he watched from a branch.

When he was hungry, Kanzi would punch "banana" on the keyboard and would lead the group to the treehouse where he knew a banana would be ready for him.

By early afternoon, the two apes were ready for a short nap. Later, Kanzi would spend an hour taking tests. One teacher would hold up three pictures, the second teacher would punch the symbol for water, and Kanzi would correctly pick out the picture of a running faucet. The test would be repeated many times with other pictures.

At 7:00 P.M., Kanzi and Mulika joined their mother in the sleeping room. Once he had gotten into bed, he used the keyboard to ask for things he was unwilling to fetch himself, such as his ball or more blankets. Most evenings, he asked to watch television. His favorite show was one of Jane Goodall studying chimpanzees in Africa. Other favorites were boxing matches and a movie pairing Clint Eastwood with a trained orangutan.

By 7:45, Kanzi and Mulika, nestled in bed, would fall asleep, and their teachers could tiptoe away, finished with another day of easy play— and hard science.

1. **Which of these sentences best tells the *main idea* of the story?**

   a. Chimpanzees can learn to associate symbols with objects only after long training.
   b. Kanzi demonstrated that chimpanzees can "pick up" language the way human children do.
   c. With the right training, animals can learn to express themselves just as people do.
   d. Since animals cannot reproduce some human sounds, they need to use another system of communication.

2. **Read the paragraph that tells about the tests that were given to Kanzi. Do you think these tests showed that Kanzi was learning language? Why or why not? Discuss this question with your partner, then write your answer on your paper.**

3. **Pet dogs often learn to respond to such sentences as "Do you want to go out?" or "Roll over." How is this similar to what Kanzi learned? How is it different? Discuss these questions with your partner. Then write your answers on your paper.**

Listening

Carlos is looking for a roommate. He is going to interview several people who are interested in sharing his apartment. The list below shows some of the things he will ask these people about. Copy the list on your paper. Then listen to the interview between Carlos and David, the first applicant to be Carlos's roommate, and take notes about David's answers.

What does David do?
What are David's hobbies?
Does David have a pet?
Does David have money for rent?

How long has David lived in the city?
When does David go to bed and get up?
What does David cook for meals?
Will David help with cleaning?

Now use your notes to ask and answer with your partner.

> A: Carlos asked David what he did. What did David answer?
> B: He said he was unemployed.

Practice Points

1. **Read each example of direct speech below and rewrite it on your paper as reported speech. Follow the example.**

(Direct speech)   The coach told the boys, "Football is a great game."

(Reported speech) *The coach told the boys that football was a great game.*

   a. Peg and Mary said, "We are having a great time."
   b. The actor told the reporter, "I start work at the studio at 7:00 o'clock every morning."
   c. Marco answered the teacher, "I have the book with that story."
   d. The doctor said to Mrs. Romero, "You can see another doctor and get a second opinion if you want to."
   e. The neighbors called me and said, "Your music is too loud, you should turn it down."

2. **Now read the sentences below and change the reported speech to direct speech.**

(Reported speech)   The teacher warned the students not to make any noise.

(Direct speech) *The teacher warned the students, "Don't make any noise."*

   a. The police officer warned the driver not to go so fast.
   b. Pauline Moreau explained that she moved to Africa when she was fifteen.
   c. Four students complained that they didn't feel very well.
   d. Mr. Suzuki said that his books were overdue at the library.
   e. The girls agreed that they should pay for the books.

3. **Change the following questions in direct speech to reported speech.**

Mary asked her teacher, "Can I take the test later?"

Mary asked her teacher if she could take the test later.

   a. Miguel asked his employer, "Is that letter all right?"
   b. The waitress asked the diners, "Can I get you anything else?"
   c. Mr. Wong asked the class, "Do you all understand Joe's explanation?"
   d. The mechanic asked the driver, "Is the engine overheating?"
   e. The flight attendant asked the little girl, "Is your seatbelt fastened?"

4. **Change the reported speech in these sentences to questions in direct speech.**

She asked if she could borrow a pencil.

She asked, "Can I borrow a pencil?"

   a. Mr. Connors asked Miss Suarez if she needed the computer.
   b. The principal asked if everyone passed the test.
   c. My friends asked me if I wanted to stay another night.
   d. The children asked if they could watch the movie on TV.
   e. Mrs. Gold asked if anyone wanted more dinner.

COMPUTERS 6

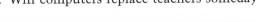

Computerized camera *Jason, Jr.* explores the *Titanic*

Discussion Points

Discuss the following questions with your classmates.

1. Do you have a home computer? What do you use it for?
2. What other things do people and society use computers for?
3. Should schools have computers?
4. Will computers replace teachers someday?

Listening

Listen to the following conversation about Martha's first computer class. Take notes so that you can discuss the following questions in class.

1. What does a floppy disk look like?
2. How should you hold a floppy disk?
3. What is a floppy disk?
4. What does the term "boot" mean?
5. What are some important rules for handling floppy disks?

Skill Points

Activity 1: Expressing opinions—pre-reading and reading exercises

Discuss the following questions with your classmates and teacher. Then read the passage below.

a. Can computers help students learn better?
b. How can computers help people in their work?
c. Can computers think the way people do?
d. Will computers be able to think in the near future?

COMPUTERS

1. What can be done with a computer? Almost anything. Computers do many things faster and better than people can. Computers never get tired and never forget information. It's almost impossible for a computer to make a mistake unless it's programmed by a human being to do so.

2. Although computers are used mainly in business, they are also very important in industry. Robotics is a new branch of computer science. It uses robots with computer brains to do many boring or dangerous jobs once performed by human beings. Some computer robots can work on assembly lines to build cars or other machinery—jobs that are boring for most people. Others do dangerous work such as putting out fires that are too hot for human fire fighters to handle.

3. Computers are also used by doctors to diagnose illnesses.

First the doctor asks detailed questions of the patient, then he or she types the answers on the computer's keyboard. In a few seconds the computer is usually able to identify the illness and to suggest an appropriate treatment.

Computers are also connected to X-ray scanners. These take thousands of pictures of the patient from a lot of different angles. At the end, the doctor can ask the computer for a picture of any organ in the body from any angle.

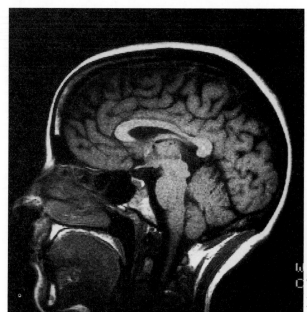

Computer scan of the brain

4. In some American schools young children are being taught by computers for part of the school day.

Before the instruction program begins, the computer asks for the student's name and identification number. Then it searches its memory to find how the student has been doing and what kind of practice is needed. The student answers the questions the computer asks by typing on a keyboard. If the answers show a good knowledge of the subject, the computer can omit a part of the lesson. If the student shows a poor knowledge of the subject, the computer can assign supplementary exercises. Students move through the material at their own speed.

5. Computers are also used to control simulators. A simulator is a training machine that duplicates, or presents an exact copy of, the conditions that a person will face on the job. For example, one simulator helps people learn how to navigate large ships such as supertankers. A room is fitted out like the bridge of a tanker, and the view through the windows is created by a computer. All the instruments and controls are connected to the computer, so that every time the pilot steers the ship the view changes accordingly. In this way, you can learn to steer a ship without taking the risk of causing a collision or running the ship aground. Aircraft pilots learn to fly in the same way.

6. Computers which can translate are being developed. It is very difficult for computers to translate from one language to another because words have different meanings in different sentences. For example, a computer needs to be given a lot of information before it can recognize the difference in meaning between "I feel like a hamburger" and "I feel like a fool." Progress is being made, however.

7. A computer can even read printed words and sentences aloud. This recent development can be especially useful to blind people. If these complicated computers can be made inexpensively, blind people may no longer need to have special "talking books" on records or tapes, or books specially printed in Braille. They may not need to find people to read to them so often. Other handicapped people are also being helped by computers.

A computer in the classroom

Research in artificial intelligence

Nearly-blind mother reads to her son

GLOSSARY

an·gles—positions
di·ag·**nose**—identify by symptoms
o·**mit**—leave out
search·es—looks for
su·per·tank·er—large ship that carries oil
sup·ple·**men**·ta·ry—extra

Activity 2: Finding the topic

Reread "Computers" and choose a correct heading for each paragraph from the list below.

Computers Teach Difficult Tasks
Computers Helping the Handicapped
The Computer *vs.* A Human Being
Computers and Medicine

Computers and Education
Computers and Foreign Languages
Computers on the Job

Activity 3: Compiling information—making a chart.

Use the topics of the paragraphs in "Computers" to fill in a chart like the one below. Also explain how the computer is used in the various fields. If you know any other use that can be made of computers, add information to the appropriate columns in the chart.

TOPICS	EXAMPLES
The Computer vs. A Human Being	Computer is faster, doesn't get tired, ...

Activity 4: Supporting the main idea

Use the information from the chart you have completed in Activity 3 to write a composition. Start your composition with this topic sentence. (A *topic sentence* gives the *main idea* of a paragraph or composition. It is usually the first sentence.)

Computers are very important in today's world.

Write the composition on your own paper. Make sure to indent the first line in each paragraph.

Activity 5: Sharing information—
pre-reading and reading

a. Before reading, discuss the following questions with your partner:

1. Can computers understand human language or do we need a special language to give them instructions?
2. What is a "computer" language?
3. Do you know any "computer" languages?

b. Read.

COMMUNICATING WITH A COMPUTER

In communicating with people, precise instructions are often not necessary. A nod of the head can mean *yes*, a wave of the hand can mean *come here*, and a very large set of "body language" cues can be understood just by gesture.

None of this is possible in our communication with the computer. Very precise instructions must be used according to pre-defined rules. When we have a problem to solve with the computer, we must carefully think through what we have to do and decide on the exact steps needed.

To help us think the problem through and to see the step-by-step procedures more clearly, we can use words and symbols in a "flow chart" form. Flow charts are an excellent way of setting out a series of instructions that must be followed in a particular order. A set of symbols has been developed for use on flow charts.

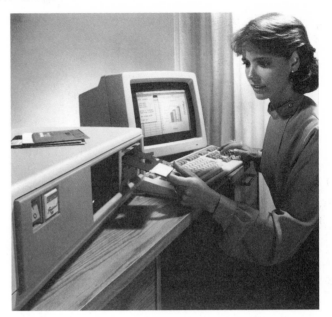

Making a flow chart helps us to think through our problem. The next step is to feed our flow chart into the computer. To do this, we must use a "computer language," a series of special commands that tell our computer what to do. When we have translated our flow chart into this language, we type it on the computer keyboard. Now when we ask questions about our problem, the computer can answer them.

c. **Reread the passage and find out which of the following statements are false.
Then rewrite them correctly on your paper.**

1. You need to be very accurate when you talk with people.
2. Communication with the computer requires a set of instructions expressed in a special way that it can understand.
3. Thinking through a problem means putting our ideas in any order to make ourselves aware of the various steps the computer has to follow to accomplish a particular task.
4. Flow charts show the steps needed to solve a problem with a computer.
5. Body language is typed on the computer keyboard so the computer can answer our questions.

Activity 6: Making a flow chart

Imagine you and your partner have run out of money and you want to get $25 for your personal expenses. You decide to go into business cutting lawns in your neighborhood. You want to cut at least five lawns and get the sum you need. You do not have a lawn mower, so you have to borrow one.

Think carefully of the various steps of the job you are going to do, discuss them with your partner and write them down in sequence. Then use these symbols to write your flowchart. At the end, compare it with the *Lawnmower Flowchart* on page 47 and discuss the differences.

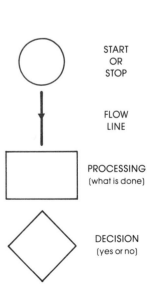

START
OR
STOP

FLOW
LINE

PROCESSING
(what is done)

DECISION
(yes or no)

Activity 7: Interpreting a flow chart

Study the flowchart on this page and answer the questions about it. Then rewrite, in the form of a paragraph, all the steps in the job that the flowchart describes. Be sure to include all the activities that this kind of job involves.

On your paper, write short answers to these questions about the flowchart.

a. According to the flowchart, what should you do if a customer doesn't want the windows washed?
b. What's the next step if the customer does want the windows washed?
c. What must you do if the windows aren't clean?
d. What do you do if they are clean?
e. What should you do if you aren't tired after the job?
f. According to the flowchart, when can you stop ringing house bells and looking for more jobs?
g. What must you do, according to the flowchart, before you stop work completely?

Literary Points

Activity 1: Alliteration

Alliteration is the repeated use of the same beginning consonant sound in words that follow closely one after another. For example in the sentence, "The mean and mischievous monkey tore the room apart merrily." the repeated sound of "**m**" in the words "mean," "mischievous," "monkey," and "merrily" create the alliteration.

Alliteration is used most often in poetry, but as an emphasizer it can be used in any form of writing, for example in fiction, essays, speeches, or drama.

Add or change words in the sentences below to create an alliteration in each one. Follow the example. Write on your paper.

The flowers grew in the garden.

The fragrant flowers grew in the great, green garden.

a. The soldiers marched into the town.
b. The wind blew the trees in the backyard.
c. The boys played a game of football.
d. The musicians played happily for the dancers.
e. The ship sailed on the water.
f. The foxes ran away from the fire.
g. The plane took off into the sky.
h. The snow fell on the streets and houses.
i. The car raced along the highway.
j. The bears danced when the trainer commanded them to.

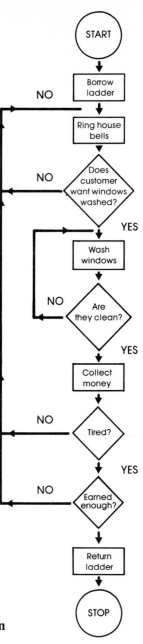

Activity 2: Reading a poem

WHO'S IN CHARGE?

by Leonard J. Soltzberg

"I make the Machine," said engineering.
"A piece of wire, a solder spot
And I will fix it before noon."

"I teach the Machine," said programming.
"A pleading word, the right command
And we'll be back to normal soon."

"I run the Machine," said operations.
"A button punched, a lever yanked
And I will have it back in tune."

"I *AM* the Machine," said a firm voice
  From the third bay,
"And *you* can all just *stew* until tomorrow!"

a. **With your partner or a small group discuss what the poet means by "engineering," "programming," and "operations." Be ready to report your conclusions to the class.**
b. **Write a short paragraph telling what you think the poet is saying in this poem. Give reasons why you think so.**

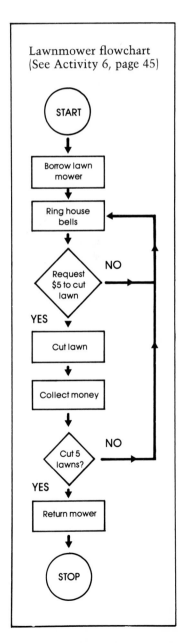

Lawnmower flowchart
(See Activity 6, page 45)

START

Borrow lawn mower

Ring house bells

Request $5 to cut lawn — NO

YES

Cut lawn

Collect money

Cut 5 lawns? — NO

YES

Return mower

STOP

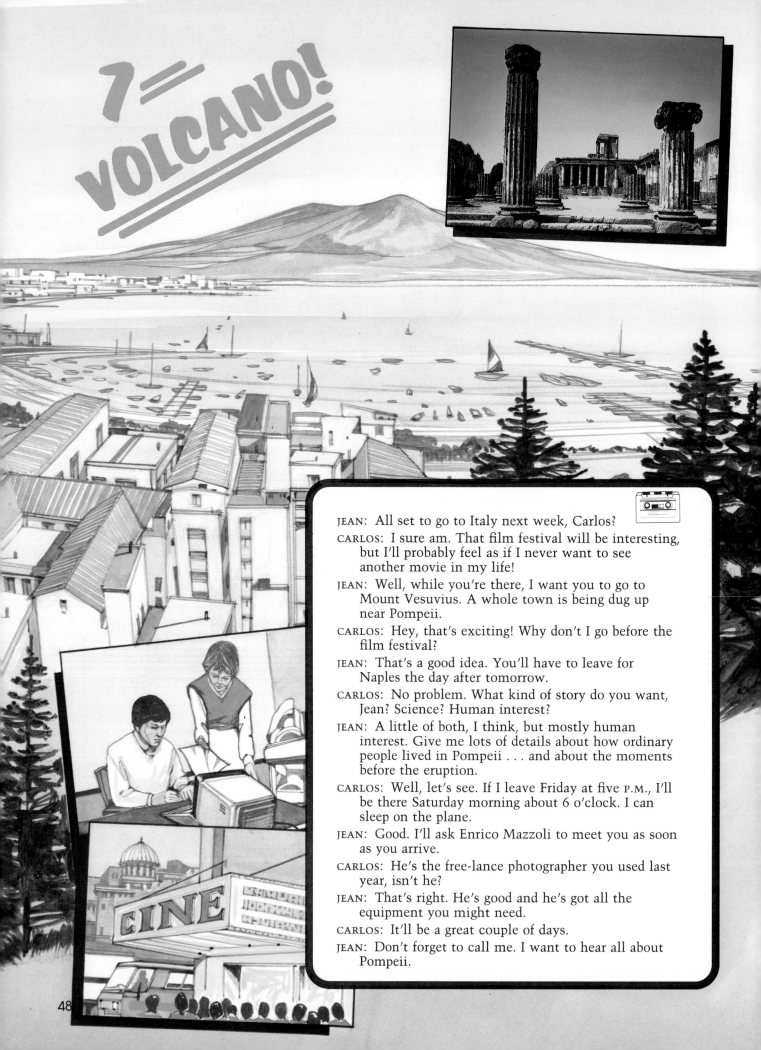

7 VOLCANO!

JEAN: All set to go to Italy next week, Carlos?

CARLOS: I sure am. That film festival will be interesting, but I'll probably feel as if I never want to see another movie in my life!

JEAN: Well, while you're there, I want you to go to Mount Vesuvius. A whole town is being dug up near Pompeii.

CARLOS: Hey, that's exciting! Why don't I go before the film festival?

JEAN: That's a good idea. You'll have to leave for Naples the day after tomorrow.

CARLOS: No problem. What kind of story do you want, Jean? Science? Human interest?

JEAN: A little of both, I think, but mostly human interest. Give me lots of details about how ordinary people lived in Pompeii . . . and about the moments before the eruption.

CARLOS: Well, let's see. If I leave Friday at five P.M., I'll be there Saturday morning about 6 o'clock. I can sleep on the plane.

JEAN: Good. I'll ask Enrico Mazzoli to meet you as soon as you arrive.

CARLOS: He's the free-lance photographer you used last year, isn't he?

JEAN: That's right. He's good and he's got all the equipment you might need.

CARLOS: It'll be a great couple of days.

JEAN: Don't forget to call me. I want to hear all about Pompeii.

Communication Points
Express conditions

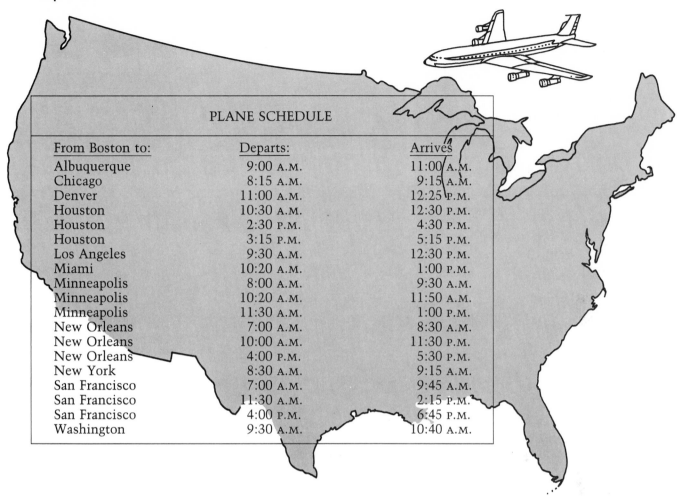

PLANE SCHEDULE		
From Boston to:	Departs:	Arrives
Albuquerque	9:00 A.M.	11:00 A.M.
Chicago	8:15 A.M.	9:15 A.M.
Denver	11:00 A.M.	12:25 P.M.
Houston	10:30 A.M.	12:30 P.M.
Houston	2:30 P.M.	4:30 P.M.
Houston	3:15 P.M.	5:15 P.M.
Los Angeles	9:30 A.M.	12:30 P.M.
Miami	10:20 A.M.	1:00 P.M.
Minneapolis	8:00 A.M.	9:30 A.M.
Minneapolis	10:20 A.M.	11:50 A.M.
Minneapolis	11:30 A.M.	1:00 P.M.
New Orleans	7:00 A.M.	8:30 A.M.
New Orleans	10:00 A.M.	11:30 P.M.
New Orleans	4:00 P.M.	5:30 P.M.
New York	8:30 A.M.	9:15 A.M.
San Francisco	7:00 A.M.	9:45 A.M.
San Francisco	11:30 A.M.	2:15 P.M.
San Francisco	4:00 P.M.	6:45 P.M.
Washington	9:30 A.M.	10:40 A.M.

You are in a travel agency in Boston. Choose one or more of the situations in column A and talk to your partner. Your partner will play the clerk's role and may choose among the sentences in column B. Continue with similar questions and answers. Then change roles.

A

a. You want to go to San Francisco tomorrow but you don't want to leave too early in the morning.

b. You want to be in Houston by 6:00 P.M. but you'll be in a meeting until 12 noon.

c. You want to be in New Orleans by 9:00 P.M., and you would like to leave in the afternoon.

d. You want to be in Minneapolis by 1:00 P.M.

B

—If you leave Boston at . . . , you'll be in . . . at . . .

—Unless you leave Boston at . . . , you won't be in . . . at . . . .

—If you don't leave Boston at . . . , you won't be in . . . at . . . .

A: I want to get to San Francisco by 1:00, but I don't want to leave too early in the morning. Can you help me?
B: I'm sorry. Unless you leave Boston at 7:00 A.M., you won't be in San Francisco at 1:00 P.M.

Ask and talk about time sequences

1. **Ask and answer questions with your partner about Carlos's trip to Italy. Use the dialogue on page 48 to find the answers. Use questions similar to these.**

   a. If Carlos leaves at 5:00 P.M., when will he arrive in Naples?
   b. What will happen as soon as he arrives?
   c. After Carlos has been to Vesuvius, who will he call?
   d. What else is Carlos going to do in Italy? When will he do it?

   > A: If Carlos leaves at 5:00 P.M., when will he arrive in Naples.
   > B: He'll arrive about 6:00 in the morning. What will happen as soon as he arrives?
   > A: . . . .

2. **Sinath Keo is a junior in high school. He likes to plan ahead, and he has made a schedule for the next ten years. Read his plan and answer the questions on your paper.**

   Ten Year Life Plan

Year	Year
1. complete 11th grade	6. graduate from college, B.S. in engineering
2. graduate from high school	7. go to work full-time
3. enter college, work part-time for Upscale Computers	8. get married
4. continue college and part-time work	9. return to school for master's degree
5. travel to Europe in summer	10. graduate with M.S. in engineering

   If Sinath follows his plan —
   a. — will he travel to Europe before or after he graduates from high school?
   b. — will he work part time when he is in college?
   c. — will he get married as soon as he graduates from college?
   d. — what will he do after he graduates from high school?
   e. — what will he do just before he gets married?
   f. — what will he do as soon as he enters college?
   g. — what will he do after he has been married for one year?

   Ask and answer questions with your partner about Sinath's life plan. Use *before*, *after*, and *as soon as* in your questions and answers.

   > A: Will Sinath work full time before he goes to college?
   > B: No, he'll work full time after he graduates from college./No, he'll work full time as soon as he graduates from college.

3. **Make a ten-year life plan for yourself. Then ask and answer questions about it with your partner, using *before*, *after*, and *as soon as*.**

   > A: Do you plan to go to college after you finish high school?
   > B: Yes, I do./No, I plan to go to work as soon as I graduate from high school.

Language Points
Reading about history
VESUVIUS: THE LAST DAYS OF POMPEII AND HERCULANEUM

Imagine living in Pompeii in A.D. 79. You are a poor fisherman or perhaps a wealthy landowner enjoying a day on the water. You are sitting in a boat when suddenly Mount Vesuvius erupts, spewing lava, ash and gases all over the western coast of Italy.

Winds quickly bear the vast cloud of ash and sulphurous steam to Pompeii. The hot air produces huge slides of mud and within hours, Pompeii—a thriving city of 20,000—has disappeared. More than 2,000 are buried beneath the rubble.

So intense was the fallout that it wasn't until the 1700s that archeologists identified the buried city and began digging out the entombed people. Skeletons of entire families were found sitting around their dinner tables, perfectly preserved and looking as if they were about to eat their evening meal. Dogs were found still on leashes and in one case, three thieves were found trying to break into a store.

The same volcanic flows that buried Pompeii and the lesser known city of Herculaneum covered the ancient beach in the Bay of Naples to a depth of 20 meters.

In the past few years a strip of that beach has been excavated, and people can descend the steep stairs to the old coast. There in the seawall of the town are ten recently uncovered chambers, probably once used to store fishing boats. In those chambers today, however, lie many well-preserved skeletons, Herculaneum's most important discoveries since the ruins were unearthed in the 18th century.

1. **There are five paragraphs in the reading. Match each of the following headings with an appropriate paragraph.**

   Bay of Naples covered by volcanic flow
   First skeletons found in Pompeii
   Chambers found in Herculaneum seawall

   Pompeii in A.D. 79
   2,000 people killed

2. **Ten words are underlined in the reading "Vesuvius: The Last Days of Pompeii and Herculaneum." Discuss these words with your partner and match them to their meanings.**

Words	Meanings
a. erupt	k. a strap or chain for holding an animal
b. spew	l. a barrier built to protect land from the sea
c. slide	m. a continuous stream of liquid or gas
d. mud	n. to pour out violently
e. rubble	o. to break open suddenly with great force
f. fallout	p. bits of broken stone, parts of buildings etc., in a pile or heap
g. entomb	
h. leash	q. small particles of material coming down from the sky
i. flow	r. rock, earth, or other material falling rapidly down the side of a hill
j. seawall	
	s. soft, wet earth
	t. to bury

3. **With your book closed, tell your partner what you remember of the reading passage. Use your own words. Remember to include these points.**

   a. year of the eruption
   b. number of people thought to have been killed
   c. cities covered by the eruption
   d. examples of skeletons found
   e. recent discoveries in the area

   Take notes on what your partner says and discuss ways in which your talks could be improved. Then check the reading to be sure that your facts were correct.

Writing

1. **Write ten sentences using the ten words in exercise 2 above. (Write a separate sentence for each word. Do not use the sentences in the reading.)**

2. **Write five sentences that *summarize*, or give the *main idea* of, the five paragraphs in the reading. Then make your sentences into a paragraph. Use the linking words, *and, but, when, so, then* to link the sentences together where you can.**

Listening

A speaker is talking about another volcanic eruption in a different part of the world. Listen to the lecture, or speech, and take notes on your paper so that you will be able to answer the following questions.

1. When were signs of the volcano first seen?
2. Who were the first people to see signs of the volcano?
3. How high was the smoke column?
4. What was the final height of the island?
5. What was the final width of the island?
6. What is the island's name?
7. To what country does the island belong?

Reading about science

WHAT CAN BONES TELL US?

To Dr. Bisel, a physical anthropologist, the beautifully preserved Herculaneum skeletons are as valuable as the treasures excavated here in the 18th century. Very few other Roman skeletons have survived; the Romans cremated their dead. Suddenly along this ancient beach lay an entire Roman population, democratically distributed among men, women, and children, patricians, freedmen, and slaves.

"These bones will have a lot to say about who these people were and how they lived," Dr. Bisel said after her first look at the site. "Take this skeleton, for example. It's a woman's skeleton. I'll determine her height by measuring one of her long bones. The state of her pelvis will tell her age and how many babies, if any, she had. I might even tell you whether she was pretty, but her face is shattered. Her bones should reveal whether she was well nourished, whether she had any of a number of diseases, and whether she had to work hard for a living. And she's just one person. There's a whole town here!"

Rick Gore, Courtesy of the National Geographic Society.

1. **With your partner, decide on meanings for each of these terms from the story. Write your meanings. Then check them with a dictionary, encyclopedia, or other reference book and correct them if you need to.**

physical anthropologist   democratically   pelvis
preserved   distributed   shattered
excavated   patricians   nourished
cremated   freedmen

2. **Write five things that can be determined from skeletons. Discuss your list with your partner. Can you think of any other things that skeletons like these might tell scientists?**

Reading fiction

THE DOG OF POMPEII

by Louis Untermeyer

Tito and his dog Bimbo lived under the wall where it joined the inner gate. They really didn't live there; they just slept there. They lived anywhere. Pompeii was one of the gayest of the old Latin towns, but although Tito was never an unhappy boy, he was not exactly a merry one. The streets were always lively with shining chariots and bright red trappings; the open-air theatres rocked with laughing crowds.

But Tito saw none of these things. He was blind—had been blind from birth. No one could say how old he was, no one remembered his parents. Bimbo was another mystery. As long as people could remember seeing Tito—they had seen Bimbo. Bimbo had never left his side.

Did I say Bimbo never left his master? I was wrong. Bimbo did trust Tito alone exactly three times a day. Early in the morning, shortly after dawn, while Tito was still dreaming, Bimbo would disappear. When Tito awoke, Bimbo would be sitting quietly at his side, a fresh-baked bread at his feet. At noon, Bimbo would put his paw on Tito's knee. Tito would curl up in the corner and go to sleep, while Bimbo would disappear again.

In half an hour he'd be back with their lunch. Sometimes it would be a piece of fruit or a scrap of meat. But sometimes there would be one of those flat, rich cakes, sprinkled with raisins and sugar, that Tito liked so much. At suppertime the same thing happened.

There was plenty of rain water in the hollows of soft stones, the old woman at the corner sometimes gave him a cupful of strong goat's milk. There was plenty of everything in Pompeii—if you had a dog like Bimbo.

As I said before, Tito was not the merriest boy in Pompeii. He could not romp with the other youngsters. But that did not make him sorry for himself. If he could not see the sights that delighted the lads of Pompeii, he could hear and smell things they never noticed. When he and Bimbo went out walking, he knew just where they were going and exactly what was happening.

"Ah," he'd sniff and say, as they passed a handsome villa. "They're going to have three kinds of bread, and a great stew." And Bimbo would note that this would be a good place to visit tomorrow.

Or, as they neared the Forum, "Mm-m! What good things they have today! Dates from Africa, and honey, and sweet onions." And so the two of them entered the center of Pompeii.

The Forum was the part of the town to which everybody came at least once during the day. It was the Central Square, and everything happened there. The buildings looked as if they were new—which, in a sense, they were. The earthquake of twelve years ago had brought down all the old structures and the citizens of Pompeii had seized the opportunity to rebuild the whole town.

Tito had heard a great deal about the earthquake. It had been a light one—as earthquakes go. There was little loss of life. No one knew what caused these earthquakes. Everyone had a different explanation.

They were talking about it this afternoon as Tito and Bimbo came out of the side street into the public square.

"I tell you," rumbled a deep voice, "there won't be another earthquake in my lifetime or yours. Earthquakes, like lightning, never strike twice in the same place."

"Do they not?" asked a thin voice Tito had never heard. "How about the two towns that have been ruined three times by the eruptions of Mount Etna? And does that column of smoke above Vesuvius mean nothing?"

"That?" Tito could hear the grunt with which one question answered another. "That's always there."

"Yes, yes," cut in the edged voice. "But the column of smoke seems hundreds of feet higher than usual, and it's thickening and spreading like a shadowy tree. And when the smoke tree above Vesuvius grows to the shape of an umbrella pine, look to your lives."

The quick shuffle of feet told Tito the stranger had gone.

"Now what," said the deep voice, "did he mean by that? I wonder. . . ."

Tito wondered, too. By nightfall the argument had been forgotten. If the smoke had increased, no one saw it in the dark. The town was in a holiday mood. Tito and Bimbo were among the merrymakers. They visited the city walls, where countless colored torches were burned. Though the thrill of lighted skies was lost to Tito, the cheers excited him as much as any, and he cried out with the loudest of them.

The next morning there were two of his beloved raisin and sugar cakes for breakfast. Bimbo was unusually active, thumping his bit of a tail. Tito could not imagine whether Bimbo was urging him to some sort of game or was trying to tell him something. Tito felt drowsy. There was a heavy mist in the air—no, a thick fog rather than a mist—a fog that got into his throat and scraped it and made him cough. He went to sleep before dusk.

He woke early. Or, rather, he was pulled awake. Bimbo had dragged him to his feet and was urging the boy along. Somewhere. Where, Tito did not know. For a while he noticed nothing except that it was hard to breathe. The air was hot. And heavy. The air, it seemed, had turned to powder—a warm powder that stung his nostrils and burned his sightless eyes.

Then he began to hear sounds. Peculiar sounds. Like animals under the earth. There was no doubt about it now. The noises came from underneath. He not only heard them—he could feel them. The earth twitched. Then the ground jerked away from his feet, and he was thrown against a stone fountain.

The water—hot water—splashing in his face revived him. He got to his feet, Bimbo steadying him, helping him on again. The noises grew louder; now they came from human throats. A few people began to rush by. Then, it seemed, an army. Time was lost in a nightmare.

It was then the crashing began. Lightnings above were answered by thunders beneath. A house fell. Then another. The two companions had escaped the dangerous side streets and were in a more open space. It was the Forum.

Tito had no idea of the time of day. He could feel it was black—an unnatural blackness. Something inside—perhaps the lack of breakfast and lunch—told him it was past noon. But nothing seemed to matter. He was getting too drowsy to walk. But walk he must. He knew it. And Bimbo knew it; the sharp tugs told him so. The ground of the Forum was safe no longer. As they stumbled out of the square, the earth wriggled like a caught snake. To walk was not enough now. They must run. Tito had lost all sense of direction. He started to go back to the inner gate, but Bimbo almost pulled his clothes from him. What did the creature want?

Then suddenly, he understood. Bimbo was telling him the way out—the sea gate—and then the sea. He turned, Bimbo guiding him.

It was growing harder and harder to breathe. It was all dust now—dust and pebbles, pebbles as large as beans, stones from the black heart of Vesuvius. The mountain was turning itself inside out.

Suddenly Tito could not go on. He staggered toward the side of the road and fell. Bimbo was beside him. He coaxed. But there was no answer. Then Bimbo did the last thing he could—the last thing he wanted to do. He bit his comrade deep in the arm. With a cry of pain, Tito jumped to his feet. Bimbo drove the boy on, snapping at his

heels. Sick with hunger, half dead with fear, Tito pounded on, pursued by Bimbo. At last he staggered through the marine gate and felt soft sand under him. Then he fainted . . . .

Someone was dashing sea water over him. Someone was carrying him toward a boat.

"Bimbo!" he called. But Bimbo had disappeared.

The boat rode over toppling waves. Tito was safe. But he wept continually.

"Bimbo!" he wailed. "Bimbo! Bimbo!"

He could not be comforted.

Eighteen hundred years passed. Scientists were excavating the ancient city. Much had already been brought to light—statues, household articles, even delicate paintings had been preserved by the fall of ashes that had taken over two thousand lives. The Forum was beginning to emerge.

"Come here," the Director called to his assistant. "I think we've discovered the remains of a building in good shape. Here is a whole wall standing with shelves inside it. Why! It must have been a bakery. And here's a curious thing. What do you think I found under this heap where the ashes were the thickest? The skeleton of a dog!"

"Amazing!" gasped his assistant. "You'd think a dog would have had sense enough to run away at the time. And what is that flat thing he's holding between his teeth?"

"It must have come from this bakery. It looks to me like some sort of cake. And if those little black pebbles aren't raisins! A raisin cake almost two thousand years old! I wonder what made him want it at such a moment?"

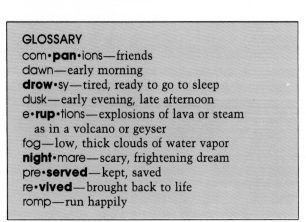

GLOSSARY
com•**pan**•ions—friends
dawn—early morning
drow•sy—tired, ready to go to sleep
dusk—early evening, late afternoon
e•**rup**•tions—explosions of lava or steam
   as in a volcano or geyser
fog—low, thick clouds of water vapor
night•mare—scary, frightening dream
pre•**served**—kept, saved
re•**vived**—brought back to life
romp—run happily

1. **Answer these questions on your paper.**

   a. How was Tito different from the other boys of Pompeii?
   b. How did Tito get his meals?
   c. Why weren't the people of Pompeii afraid of another earthquake?
   d. Where did Bimbo pull Tito?
   e. Why did Bimbo bite Tito?
   f. At the end of the story, where did Bimbo go? Why?
   g. How did Tito feel as the boat pulled away?

2. **Discuss the following questions with the class or a small group. Then write your final answers on your paper.**

   a. The *setting* of a story is the place and time of the story. What is the setting of this story? How does the setting change at the end of the story?
   b. How do you think Bimbo got the food he brought to Tito?
   c. Which of the two parts of the story is more likely to be based on fact—the story of Tito and Bimbo or the story of the Director and the assistant? Explain your answer.

Writing

What will happen to Tito? Write a composition that describes who Tito meets on the boat, where he goes, how he lives, and who takes care of him. Use your imagination to create an interesting future for him. Before writing, talk with your partner and other classmates about the topic. Write down as many ideas as you can including ideas and information you get from others. Arrange your ideas. Then write a first draft. Be ready to share this first draft with your class or group and listen to any criticisms and suggestions they may have. When you prepare your final draft, be careful to include your classmates' suggestions, if you agree with them, and any corrections in spelling and grammar that they or your teacher may have pointed out.

Practice Points

1. **Complete the following sentences on your paper. Use: *if, in case, unless, as soon as.***

   a. . . . they don't close that window, it will get cold in here.
   b. . . . the children are good, I won't baby-sit for them.
   c. . . . you get to the New York airport, you'll meet your parents.
   d. . . . you don't catch the 9 o'clock bus, I've given you enough money to take a taxi.
   e. . . . she reads that book, she'll understand more about computers.
   f. We won't wait . . . you are late.
   g. She won't learn English . . . she goes to the United States or England.
   h. . . . I hear the bell, I'll open the door.
   i. Mary won't write to Jim again . . . he writes to her first.
   j. I'm going to take my umbrella this morning . . . it rains this afternoon.

2. **Complete the following sentences any way you like, but be sure your sentences make sense.**

   a. I will go to the movies if . . . .
   b. My mother won't give me anything unless . . . .
   c. In case I can't finish my homework . . . .
   d. As soon as I finish school . . . .
   e. If I'm free on Saturday afternoon . . . .
   f. Unless my friend doesn't study hard . . . .
   g. As soon as I am 20 . . . .
   h. In case I get some money for my birthday . . . .
   i. If I go to the library . . . .
   j. I don't like fish unless . . . .

8 Talking About Language

國 country

中 middle

美 beautiful

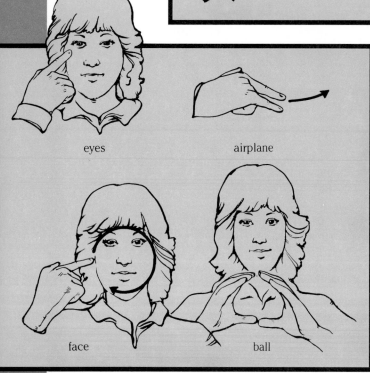

eyes

airplane

face

ball

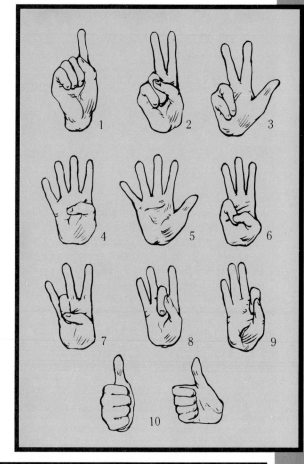

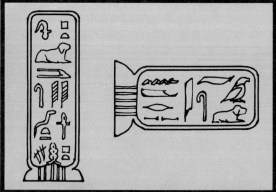

Braille

a	b	c	d	e	f	g
h	i	j	k	l	m	n
o	p	q	r	s	t	u
v	w	x	y	z		

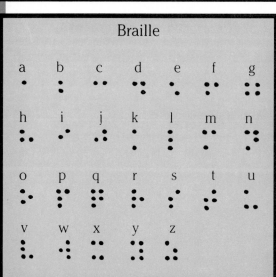

Discussion Points

The illustrations above show different ways of communicating, that is, ways for one person to pass information to another person. Talk with your partner and see whether you can figure out what they are. How are they used? Who uses them? What are the differences between the way you communicate and the ways these are used?

Listening

Activity 1. Matching definitions

Before listening to the lecture, do the following activity.
On your paper match items from column A with their definitions in Column B.

A

a. alphabet
b. hieroglyphs
c. Louis Braille
d. gesture
e. sign language
f. Roman alphabet
g. blind
h. deaf

B

i. the series of letters used to write English and many other languages
j. unable to hear
k. a group of signs or symbols used to make words, each one standing for a letter or a sound or sounds
l. unable to see
m. inventor of reading and writing system for the blind
n. any expressive movement of hand or body
o. Egyptian picture writing
p. a form of language used by people who cannot hear

Activity 2. True or false

Listen to the lecture. On your paper mark these statements True or False. Rewrite the false ones so that they are correct.

a. All languages use the Roman alphabet.
b. Hieroglyphic writing is used in Egypt today.
c. The word "alphabet" comes from two Greek words.
d. Typewriters for Chinese are much more complicated than typewriters for English.
e. Sign language can only express numbers and motions.

Skill Points

Activity 1: Reading for information and discussion

HOW DO WE LEARN OUR LANGUAGE?

An old and often-told joke in the United States goes something like this: "People in China must be terribly intelligent! They all learn to speak Chinese with no difficulty at all!"

In fact, acquiring language is the most natural thing in the world for most human beings. Unless their brain has been damaged, nearly all children learn whatever language—or languages—they hear spoken around them. Many children grow up speaking more than one language, and some children speak four or five languages. This kind of learning goes on without any apparent effort or hard work.

Language learning starts in the first months of life. Most of us have heard babies "babbling," that is, making all kinds of nonsense sounds. Although these babies are not saying words, they are practicing the sounds of language. As they hear language spoken around them, they practice the sounds of that language.

When adults, grown people, learn a new language, it is usually very hard for them to learn to make all the new sounds correctly. But babies effortlessly learn to make every kind of sound that their language uses. Soon they learn to combine these sounds into words which are attached to meanings. There may be a few sounds that they find hard to say until their voice muscles are older, but mostly they pronounce their words correctly.

Language is much more than sounds or words, of course. Each language has a grammar or a structure, that is, a way in which the words are put together. The child learns this structure, too. By the time you were three years old, you had learned to use most of the grammar of your language. There were some fine points that you did not learn until later, and there were many words that you had not learned yet, but you knew the basics of your language. You knew the order in which words are used, for example. An English speaking child learns to say "the blue sky" while a French-speaking child says "le ciel bleu."

In short, you learned to speak the way the people around you spoke. But what happens to children who do not get the usual language experience? A blind child will still acquire the language that is heard. It is what is taken through the ears that is most important. The child's blindness is not a problem in learning language until it is time to learn to read. Then the child will need to learn by the system of raised dots called Braille instead of flat print. But the child will already know the vocabulary and grammar that are used in his or her own family.

For a deaf child, the story is very different. It is impossible for a child who is born deaf to acquire language through sound. This is a very serious problem. It is much harder for deaf children to learn how the language of their culture works than it is for children who can hear. And to learn to speak, after they have found out what "words" are, they must watch other people's mouths and feel the vibrations of the vocal cords in their own and in other people's throats.

Many deaf persons learn to communicate by sign language, using their hands to show ideas and actions. Sign language, like spoken language, can explain whatever people want to say. Sometimes when you watch a speech on television, you will see a small picture in the corner of the screen where a user of sign language "tells" deaf people what is being said. (Many television programs have the words that are being spoken printed at the bottom of the screen. A special attachment on the TV set makes it possible to see the words.)

Schools for deaf people may teach sign language or may teach the deaf to speak and to understand others by watching their mouths when they speak. Gallaudet College in Washington, D.C., is the only liberal arts college specifically for deaf people

Computer class conducted in sign language at Gallaudet College

in the world. At Gallaudet, students learn both spoken language and sign language.

Now imagine what it is like to be both blind and deaf. There is no sound to carry a message to you. You cannot see other people talking to each other. How do you learn that "language" exists? It is very, very hard, and not many people have been able to succeed in entering the speaking world from the deaf and blind world.

Helen Keller was a woman of great courage who fought to overcome the wall of deafness and blindness which cut her off from life. When we read her story, we see that the biggest problem was right at the beginning—she did not have any idea of "words." And that is the most exciting moment of all in her story—when she first understood how meaning went from one person to another.

Helen Keller's story called attention to the problem of teaching deaf-blind children. Because of her example, the seeing and hearing world realized that these children could learn to use language and join the rest of society. Her experience added to our understanding of how everyone acquires language.

GLOSSARY
ac·**quire**—to learn, to take possession of
ap·**par**·ent—noticeable, obvious
com·**bine**—to put together
dam·aged—hurt, broken
vi·**bra**·tions—shaking movements

Talk about the following questions in class, then use the ideas you have discussed to write answers on your paper.

a. There are three other senses besides the sense of sight (seeing) and hearing. What are they?

b. Do you think some languages are more difficult than others? What are they? Which languages seem easy, which ones hard? Why?

c. What are some of the first words children learn to say in your language?

d. Do you know what your first words were? Ask your parents what they were. How old were you when you began to speak? Find out from your parents or an older relative.

e. Does English sometimes seem "reversed" to you? Which pattern does your language use to describe a noun, "blue sky" or "sky blue"? Tell about other differences between your language and English.

f. Imagine for some reason that you have to give up either your sense of sight or your sense of hearing. Which would you choose to give up and why?

Activity 2: Scanning for specific facts

To *scan* means to read quickly to find one or more specific facts. Scan this short biography of Helen Keller to find answers to these questions. Write the answers on your paper.

a. In what state did Helen Keller live as a child?
b. What kind of illness did Helen Keller have?
c. In what city did Annie Sullivan go to school?
d. Who lived in the same house at school with Annie Sullivan?
e. What is the manual alphabet?
f. What happened to make the idea of language enter Helen's mind?
g. What did Helen "set her heart on"?
h. What did Helen call Annie Sullivan?
i. Where did Helen go to college and when did she graduate?
j. What was Helen's most important gift to the world?

HELEN KELLER—an Extraordinary Person

The little girl was more like a wild animal than a child. She would throw herself on the floor and kick and scream. No one knew how to help her understand the life around her.

The little girl's name was Helen Keller, and she was seven years old. Helen was born in Alabama in 1881. She was a bright and beautiful child. But when she was less than two years old, she became ill with a terrible fever. When she recovered from her illness, she had lost her sight, her hearing, and her speech. Her parents took Helen to many doctors, hoping that someone could do something for their beloved daughter.

Nothing could be done to restore Helen's sight or hearing. But the Perkins School for the Blind in Boston, Massachusetts, said that they could send a teacher who might be able to help her. The teacher, Annie Sullivan, had just graduated from Perkins. She was an orphan who had been blind.

Helen Keller and Anne Sullivan

She had learned to read Braille. Then later her sight had been partially restored through an operation.

Annie had lived in the same house at Perkins with Laura Bridgman who, like Helen Keller, was both deaf and blind. Annie had seen how the manual alphabet was used to speak with Laura. The manual alphabet is a way of making letters with one's hand. Annie saw that Laura was able to feel the letters as her teacher made them into Laura's hand. Now Annie was to go to Alabama to lead Helen Keller into the world.

The first and hardest thing to do was to make a link in Helen's mind between words and the world she touched, but could not see or hear. With love and patience, Annie spelled words into Helen's hand while Helen touched the object which was being named. Helen Keller wrote in her autobiography of the day on which she suddenly became aware of the connection between the hand spelling and the objects, the day on which *language* entered her mind.

Helen Keller was a very brilliant woman. She was also a very determined person. She set her heart on being able to speak, even though she could not hear. It is very difficult for someone to learn speech who cannot hear it. It was a hard, frustrating battle, but she won it. Her speech was not very clear, but it was understandable. It meant she could talk to people directly, quickly, without the slow spelling of letters into someone's hand.

Annie Sullivan was Helen's link with the world. Helen felt that she could not have accomplished the things she did without the help of "Teacher," the name she used for Annie Sullivan. With Annie Sullivan's help, Hellen Keller became a well-educated person. She read constantly, and studied foreign languages and science. Annie read many books for her that were not printed in Braille. Helen said that she found geometry the most difficult subject to learn because it was necessary for her to remember the shapes as she did the problems.

Helen wanted to go to college. She was able to persuade Radcliffe College, a women's college associated with Harvard University in Massachusetts, to admit her. The college staff did not believe that Helen could do college work, but she graduated in 1904 with high honors. Annie Sullivan was at her side as Helen received her diploma at graduation.

The books that Helen Keller wrote, and the lectures that she gave, changed the way people viewed deaf and blind people. The world came to understand that Helen Keller's blindness and deafness did not limit the greatness of her heart and mind.

GLOSSARY

ad·mit—to let (someone) into a place or institution

bril·liant—smart, intelligent

de·ter·mined—firm, strong in achieving a particular purpose

ill—sick

link—connection

per·suade—to talk (someone) into believing or taking action

re·store—to make like new, to give (something) back

Activity 3: Reading an autobiography

A *biography* is the story of somebody's life. An *autobiography* is a special kind of biography. It is the story of a person's life told by that person. Read the following passage and answer the questions about it.

THE STORY OF MY LIFE

From Helen Keller's autobiography

The morning after my teacher came she led me into her room and gave me a doll. The little blind children at the Perkins Institution had sent it and Laura Bridgman had dressed it; but I did not know this until afterward. When I had played with it a little while, Miss Sullivan slowly spelled into my hand the word "d-o-l-l." I was at once interested in this finger play and tried to imitate it. When I finally succeeded in making the letters correctly, I was flushed with childish pleasure and pride. Running downstairs to my mother, I held up my hand and made the letters for doll. I did not know that I was spelling a word or even that words existed; I was simply making *my* fingers go in monkey-like imitation. . . .

One day, while I was playing with my new doll, Miss Sullivan put my big rag doll into my lap also, spelled "d-o-l-l" and tried to make me understand that "d-o-l-l" applied to both. Earlier in the day we had had a tussle over the words "m-u-g" and "w-a-t-e-r." Miss Sullivan had tried to impress it upon me that "m-u-g" is *mug* and "w-a-t-e-r" is *water*, but I persisted in confounding the two. In despair she had dropped the subject for the time, only to renew it at the first opportunity. . . .

We walked down the path to the well house, attracted by the fragrance of the honeysuckle with which it was covered. Someone was drawing water and my teacher placed my hand under the spout. As the cool stream gushed over one hand she spelled into the other the word *water*, first slowly, then rapidly. I stood still, my whole attention fixed upon the motions of her fingers. Suddenly I felt a misty consciousness as of something forgotten—a thrill of returning thought; and somehow the mystery of language was revealed to me.

I knew then that "w-a-t-e-r" meant the wonderful cool something that was flowing over my hand. That living word awakened my soul, gave it light, hope, joy, set it free! . . .

I left the well-house eager to learn. Everything had a name, and each name gave birth to a new thought. As we returned to the house every object which I touched seemed to quiver with life. That was because I saw everything with the strange new sight that had come to me.

Answer these questions on your paper. You can reread the biography on page 61 as well as Helen Keller's own description in her autobiography.

a. Why did Helen Keller think that it was important to tell her readers that Laura Bridgman had dressed the doll that Annie Sullivan brought with her to Alabama?

b. Helen says, "Miss Sullivan had tried to impress it upon me that 'm-u-g' is *mug* and that 'w-a-t-e-r' is *water*, but I persisted in confounding the two." Does this sentence show that Helen was almost to the point of learning language? Why or why not? How was it different from the experience by the well?

c. What was "the strange new sight that had come to me"? Why do you think Helen chose to use the words "saw" and "sight" in talking about her experience?

d. Helen says that when she made the connection between the water on her hand and the finger spelling of w-a-t-e-r, there was a feeling "as of something forgotten—a thrill of returning thought." What was the "something forgotten"? How did the fact that she had once known how to speak (before she was two years old) help her learn now?

e. Helen uses several words in this passage that may be unfamiliar to you. Find these words and write a meaning for each one based on the way it is used. Then look the words up in your dictionary and correct your meanings if you need to. These are the words.

imitate (paragraph 1)   despair (paragraph 2)
flushed (paragraph 1)   gushed (paragraph 3)
pride (paragraph 1)   consciousness (paragraph 3)
applied (paragraph 2)   revealed (paragraph 3)
tussle (paragraph 2)   quiver (paragraph 4)
confounding (paragraph 2)

Literary Points

Activity 1: Word study—slang

Slang words or expressions are popular, temporary language. Sometimes they are not even in the dictionary. Slang does not usually stay popular for very long. It may disappear after a while, or it may be accepted into standard language. Often the slang words are standard words with a new meaning. For example,

That's super! = That's very, very good!
The word "super" is usually a prefix, used before other words to mean "higher, over." A "supersonic plane" is a plane that flies at speeds greater than the speed of sound.

Here are some slang words that have been popular in the recent past. On your paper, choose the meaning from column B that matches the slang expression in column A. The answers are at the bottom of the page upside down.

A	B
a. Cool it.	e. right in style
b. That's awesome.	f. makes you want to dance
c. He's a cool cat.	g. calm down, don't get excited
d. That music's groovy.	h. wonderful, terrific

Activity 2: Mood

Very often when talking about literature, people speak of the mood of a story, poem, or novel. The *mood* (sometimes called the *tone*) simply means the feeling the author communicates through his or her words. Effective writing puts the reader into the same mood as the story. Sometimes the mood of a passage is good and positive, but other times a story can have a negative or unhappy mood.

Below are listed some words that are used to describe the mood of prose and poetry. Find the *antonym* (opposite) for each negative word in column A, with a positive word in column B. Write the word pairs on your paper.

A

a. serious
b. heavy
c. sad
d. solemn
e. dull
f. pessimistic
g. despairing

B

h. optimistic
i. gay
j. hopeful
k. comical
l. happy
m. light
n. lively

Activity 3: Reading a poem

MIMI'S FINGERS

by Mary O'Neill

I am blind. All that I can see
My enchanted fingers bring to me,
As if all sight were mingled with all touch
I do not mind not-seeing very much.
In Braille I read the words these fingers trace,
And with them come to know your smile, your face,
Your buckled shoes, the silk-thread of your hair,
The fabric of each suit and dress you wear;
All shapes, all sizes, how long, how far, how high,
How round a bowl, how gently curved the sky,
How pointed the far tip-top of a hill,
The narrow table of a window sill.
I know a snowflake as a melting star,
The sticky-thick of honey and tar.
Color alone my fingers cannot do.
Could you, could you, tell me about blue?

Work with a partner to answer these questions.

a. How does Mimi, the speaker in the poem, "see" the world?
b. What does Mimi mean when she says, "I do not mind not-seeing very much"?
c. Which words rhyme in this poem?
d. What can Mimi's fingers NOT do?
e. How could you explain colors to a blind person? Are there certain objects which are like colors and give body to the abstract idea of colors? Think of objects which represent the six basic colors: green, blue, red, yellow, black, and white.

9 DISASTER!

CHANNEL 8

BARBARA: I watched your program on the *Titanic* last night. It was really good!

CARLOS: Well, of course, none of it was terribly new, but I thought it was a pretty good summary of what's been found out.

BARBARA: So did I. Carlos, what would you do if you were in a shipwreck?

CARLOS: I'd dress warmly! Most of the big shipwrecks have happened during cold weather. And ocean water is almost always cold.

BARBARA: I hadn't thought of that.

CARLOS: A lot of the people who didn't survive the big shipwrecks died from freezing, not from drowning.

BARBARA: You must have done a lot of research!

CARLOS: Both Jean and I did. We read books, magazines, newspaper articles, and official reports. And I interviewed people.

BARBARA: Do women and children really get saved first the way people say they do?

CARLOS: It's hard to say. It starts out that way but when the ship finally goes down, people are likely to worry about themselves instead of others. But many people turn out to be true heroes in a disaster.

BARBARA: What about the saying that the captain always goes down with the ship?

CARLOS: That really is what usually happens.

BARBARA: Carlos, would you actually go down with your ship if you were captain?

CARLOS: Of course. I'm as sure of that as I am that I'll get fired if I don't get to the studio on time!

Communication Points
Ask and talk about hypothetical situations

1. **A** *hypothetical situation* **is a "what if . . ." or "imagine that . . ." situation. It is a situation that is not true for you but that can be imagined to be true. Here are some hypothetical situations. How would you get out of these? Choose one of the three answers each time and write its number on your paper. Do all the situations. Then talk about them with your partner.**

What would you do if . . .

a. you were lost in the woods?
   1. start to walk straight ahead
   2. turn around and follow my tracks backward
   3. sit down and wait for help

b. a poisonous snake bit you?
   1. run to the nearest hospital
   2. hold a lighted match to the bite
   3. tie a tight rope above the bite and then suck the poison from it

c. you had to light a fire and you didn't have any matches?
   1. strike a piece of wood and a stone against each other
   2. rub two pieces of wood together
   3. hold some dried leaves in the sunlight

d. you wanted to find out which way to go home and you didn't have a compass?
   1. watch the way the sun moved
   2. find which way the wind was blowing
   3. watch which direction the birds were flying

e. you wanted to find your way at night?
   1. look at the moon, because the curve points north
   2. wait till morning when the sun comes up
   3. look for the North Star

f. you were in a desert and you didn't have any water?
   1. try to reach the nearest oasis where there is always water
   2. cut a hole in a cactus plant
   3. dig down in the sand until I hit water

g. you found water and you didn't know if it was safe to drink?
   1. boil it for 20 minutes
   2. pour it through a handkerchief to filter out the dirt
   3. let it stand for 24 hours so the dirt would settle out

h. you fell into a river and you couldn't swim?
   1. wave my hands to attract someone's attention
   2. shout for help
   3. lie on my back with my mouth out of water and my arms under the water and breathe deeply

> A: If I was lost in the woods, I'd . . . .
> B: I'd do the same thing./I wouldn't. I'd . . . .

2. **With your partner, check your answers against those on page 68. One of you reads answer *a* aloud, the others reads answer *b*, and so on. See who has the larger number of right answers. Then, without looking at the text, explain to your partner why some of his or her answers are wrong.**

a. 2. When you walk in the woods it is very hard to tell your direction. You usually turn slightly to the right, and walk in a wide circle. If you are lost, the best thing to do is to keep calm and try to follow your tracks backwards.

b. 3. When a poisonous snake bites you, the poison spreads through the body by means of the blood circulation. So it is important not to exercise, in order to keep your heart from beating rapidly and moving the blood and snake poison through your body. The first thing to do is to tighten a rope or belt around the arm or leg above the bite. Then cut the bite to make it bleed. You can also suck the blood from the snake bite, as the poison is not harmful when it is swallowed.

c. 2. You can light a fire using two pieces of wood, the way American Indians used to. Turn a stick of hard wood rapidly back and forth against a hollowed out piece of soft wood. This will eventually produce sparks.

d. 1. If you don't have a compass, the sun can show you the direction. In the northern hemisphere the sun is in the east at six A.M., at noon it is in the south, and at six P.M. it is in the west. In the southern hemisphere the sun is in the north at noon.

e. 3. The North Star (or Pole Star) is the last star in the Little Dipper. While all the other stars and constellations rotate, the North Star remains pointing north. In the southern hemisphere the North Star cannot be seen. The Southern Cross, a constellation of four stars, points south.

f. 2. Cactus is a plant found in dry, hot regions. This plant stores up water which you can drink in an emergency.

g. 1. The easiest way to make water safe to drink is to boil it for at least 20 minutes. This kills all the bacteria that might be in the water.

h. 2. If you can't swim and you fall into deep water, remember that you will not sink if you can keep your mouth out of the water by throwing back your head. Keep your lungs full of air by breathing out as little air as possible. Keep your arms under the water; it is easier to float that way.

Ask for and give advice

1. **Imagine you found yourself in each of these situations. What would you do? Write your answers on your paper.**

   a. Tomorrow is your friend's birthday. You want to get a present but you don't know what your friend would like.
   b. You have received a gift of money from one of your relatives.
   c. You found a puppy in the street and it has followed you home.
   d. You have quarrelled with your best friend but you want to be friends again.
   e. You found a wallet in the street that contains money.
   f. You lent a book to a friend but the friend hasn't returned it yet.
   g. Someone you like is going to give a party but you haven't been invited.
   h. One of your classmates thinks you said something unfriendly, and now won't talk to you.

2. **Now work with your partner. Ask for and give advice. Use the situations in exercise 1 and add others that you think of yourself. Then change roles.**

   A: Tomorrow is my friend's birthday. What should I get for a present?
   B: If I were you I'd get . . . .
   A: That's a good idea./No, I'd rather get . . . .

Language Points
Reading about history

THE LAST NIGHT OF THE *TITANIC*

She was announced as the world's "safest ship" and unsinkable because of her new system of watertight doors.

She was the *Titanic*, pride of the White Star Line, embarked from Southampton, England, on April 10, 1912, for her first voyage across the North Atlantic to New York.

The liner boasted the new wireless radio, a theater, tennis and squash courts, Turkish baths, four restaurants plus the main dining room, a miniature golf course, and a dog kennel. What more could her passengers ask for?

More than 1,500 passengers would enjoy these splendid accommodations on the *Titanic's* inaugural crossing. In addition, more than 700 immigrants boarded her as third class passengers. Captain E. T. Smith hoped to set a new crossing record with the *Titanic* and kept his speed at twenty-two knots. He had received some warnings about icebergs in the shipping lanes, but the first five days at sea were sunny and the visibility was excellent.

On the night of April 14, the *Titanic* had entered the Grand Banks area off Newfoundland when a lookout saw an iceberg. But the warning came too late and the giant liner sideswiped the iceberg. Only a slight bump was felt, but in that brief moment the ice had fatally injured the great ship.

The *Titanic's* radio began sending SOS signals, but the signals went unanswered. Inexplicably a ship that was seen on the horizon sailed away, ignoring the radio calls as well as the signal rockets. That ship was later identified as the *Californian*. Its radio operator had turned off his radio receiver and had gone to sleep moments before the *Titanic* struck the iceberg.

Nearly an hour after the *Titanic* began taking on water, her first lifeboats were lowered. The delay was due to the fact that the liner was thought to be unsinkable. Some passengers on the saloon deck put pieces of ice from the iceberg in their glasses and went back to the dining room where an orchestra was playing.

Because of the leaning position of the ship, a number of boats could not be released from their davits. Others pulled away from the ship only half-filled with passengers. In fact both the crew and the passengers were panic-stricken.

Purser and Captain of the *Titanic*

Grand staircase of the *Titanic*

Shortly after 2:00 A.M., the *Titanic's* stern rose high above the cold waters, and in a burst of bubbles, sank beneath the waves, taking with her some 1,500 people.

Among the prominent passengers who died were Benjamin Guggenheim, Col. John Jacob Astor (although his wife survived), Frank D. Millet, a renowed American painter, William T. Stead, a leading British journalist, and Henry B. Harris, a noted Broadway producer.

Later, an official inquiry would find the White Star Line negligent, with only enough lifeboats for little more than 1100 people. The crew was also cited for lack of training and discipline. And the captain, who went down with his ship, was condemned for pushing the *Titanic* to excessive speeds despite the iceberg warnings.

Two years later, as a result of the disaster, the U.S. Coast Guard established the first iceberg patrols of the North Atlantic.

In the years after the *Titanic* disaster, many people tried to locate the sunken ship. They proposed ways of raising it, bringing it back to the surface. Some hoped to sell it for scrap metal. Others thought that there could be valuable things in the ship's safe which could be recovered and sold. But nobody knew exactly where the *Titanic* was or what condition it was in.

In September of 1985, a French-American expedition under the leadership of an American scientist, Robert Ballard, finally located the *Titanic* on the ocean bottom. A year later, Ballard headed another expedition to explore and photograph the wrecked ship. Using *Alvin*, a three-person submarine designed for exploring in very deep water, the scientists examined the whole outside of the ship, which had broken into two pieces when it sank. A small robot camera, called *Jason Jr.*, was sent into the ship to take pictures.

Until Ballard's 1986 expedition, most people believed that the iceberg had torn a 300-foot hole in the side of the *Titanic*. The expedition did not find any hole. Instead, it found that bumping against the iceberg had bent some of the steel plates that made up the ship's hull and forced them apart, allowing water to pour in.

The expedition found that the ship had badly deteriorated in the water. The steel hull was covered with rust. All the wood inside the ship had been eaten by worms. At the end of the 1986 expedition, Ballard said that he felt that the remains of the *Titanic* should be left where they were, and that no attempt should be made to salvage them.

GLOSSARY

boast·ed—was proud of

cit·ed—called to appear before a court of law to answer an accusation

dav·its—curved poles that support the lifeboats on a ship and are used to lower them

de·**te**·ri·o·ra·ted—become worse in quality or value, rotted, decayed

in·ex·**pli**·ca·bly—in a way that cannot be explained or understood

in·**au**·gu·ral—first in a planned series

knot—a measure of a ship's speed equal to 6076.12 feet per hour

lean·ing—at an angle, not upright

lin·er—a large passenger ship

look·out—a person who keeps watch on a ship

neg·li·gent—showing lack of attention or care

sal·vage—save or restore a wrecked ship or its cargo

side·swiped—hit along the side in passing

un·**sink**·a·ble—built so that it cannot sink or go to the bottom of the sea

wa·ter·tight—built so that no water can get in or through

Several circumstances caused the shipwreck of the *Titanic* and the death of hundreds of people. Match phrases from the two columns and find out what would have happened if things had gone differently. Then write the complete sentences on your paper.

A

a. More people would have been saved from the sea . . .
b. The *Californian* would have responded to the SOS . . .
c. All the lifeboats would have been filled with passengers . . .
d. The lifeboats would have been lowered an hour before . . .
e. All the lifeboats would have been lowered . . .
f. The ship would have been able to steer clear of the iceberg . . .
g. The *Californian* would have rescued all the passengers . . .
h. The captain would have gone more slowly . . .

B

i. if he had not wanted to set a new record.
j. if it had not been going so fast.
k. if the radio operator had not turned off the radio.
l. if the signal rockets had not been ignored.
m. if the ship had not been considered unsinkable.
n. if the ship had not been leaning way over.
o. if there had not been too few lifeboats.
p. if the crew had not been panic-stricken.

Listening

Listen to the story told by one of the survivors of the *Titanic* and answer the following questions on your paper.

1. How old was Mr. Drew when the *Titanic* sank?
2. Who accompanied him during the voyage?
3. What time did the *Titanic* strike the iceberg?
4. How many passengers could the lifeboats hold?
5. What happened at 2:20?

Practice Points

1. Look at the example. Then change the following sentences in the same way on your paper.

Ann wouldn't buy the rugs if she didn't like them.

Anne wouldn't buy the rugs unless she liked them.

a. Carlos wouldn't take this road if it wasn't safe.
b. We won't go to the baseball game if it doesn't stop raining.
c. You won't learn to play the guitar if you don't practice hard.
d. He wouldn't behave like that if he wasn't angry.
e. I wouldn't wear that dress if I didn't like it.
f. I don't like meat if it isn't well done.
g. He wouldn't have come if he hadn't heard some news.
h. She wouldn't help him if she didn't want to.

2. **Look at situations _a_ through _h_. For each one, choose an appropriate piece of advice from the box. Then write the situation and the advice in a dialogue.**

   a. I guess I have a little temperature.

   A: I guess I have a little temperature.

   B: If I were you, I'd stay in bed and take an aspirin.

   b. I think I forgot to lock the front door.
   c. I've spent fifty dollars to have my stereo fixed and it still doesn't work.
   d. Do you like my new haircut?
   e. Gosh! It's pouring. Do you think I should go to the store?
   f. I'm sure Mom will let me give a party for my birthday.
   g. I think my Dad is mad at me because I took the car yesterday without asking him.
   h. John keeps asking me for a date. What should I do?

Tell him you really aren't interested in him.	Change your hairdresser.
Ask for your money back.	Ask her first.
Don't go out in this weather.	Go home right away.
Stay in bed and take an aspirin.	Apologize to him.

3. **When we talk about situations that are hypothetical, we use the past tense. On your paper, rewrite these sentences changing the verb to the past tense as shown in the examples.**

   I'd buy another ice cream cone if I (have) any money.

   I'd buy another ice cream cone if I had any money.

   If it was closer, I (can/walk) to the post office.

   If it was closer, I could walk to the post office.

   a. If she (repeat) the instructions, you would understand them.
   b. I (will/show) you how it works if I had more time.
   c. This would be a great place for a picnic if it (not/be) so crowded.
   d. I'm sure your father (will/lend) you the car if it was here.
   e. If you didn't have any homework, you (can/watch) television.
   f. I (can/go) to the movies with you if I didn't have to visit my aunt.
   g. If it (not/be) raining, we could go for a walk in the park.
   h. If they knew him better, they (will/ask) him to the party.

4. **Rewrite the following sentences on your paper using the examples as a guide.**

   Jean drives more slowly than Carlos.

   Carlos doesn't drive as slowly as Jean.

   George can run faster than most fifteen-year-old boys can.

   Most fifteen-year-olds can't run as fast as George can.

   a. John is studying harder now than he did last year.
   b. Francisco speaks English more clearly than Gonzalo.
   c. Bill arrived at the party later than Glenda.
   d. My brother usually gets up earlier in the morning than my sister does.
   e. I feel better today than I did yesterday.
   f. I like fishing more than you do.
   g. I can study better in the morning than in the afternoon.
   h. We walked farther than Yuan and Charley did.
   i. Dan can sing much better than I can.

Whales and the Sea

Discussion Points

Have you had any personal adventures? Talk about them with your classmates. Do you know any exciting adventures that happened to others? Tell about them, too. Then discuss what makes people look for adventures. What "rewards" do they get from their adventures?

Listening

Listen to the story of Robin Lee Graham, a 16-year-old boy who sailed around the world alone. Take notes on your paper. After you have heard Robin's story, use your notes to talk with your partner about Robin's trip. Include the following information in your notes.

1. the names of several of the places that Robin visited
2. the problems Robin had at sea
3. the oceans that Robin sailed on
4. the length of time it took Robin to make the journey

Robin Lee Graham on *Dove*

Skill Points

Activity 1: Reading to predict outcomes and draw conclusions

a. **Before you read "I Touched a Whale," discuss these questions with your partner.**

1. From the story's title, what do you think it will be about?
2. Where do whales generally live?
3. What length can a whale reach?

b. **Look at the drawing of a humpback whale and notice the labels. Watch for some of these words in the reading.**

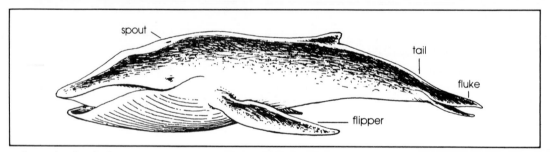

A humpback whale

c. **Look at the maps. Notice that the map on the right is an enlargment of a small part of the map on the left. As you read the story, use the maps to find out where it took place.**

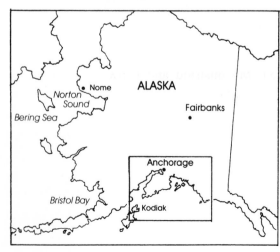

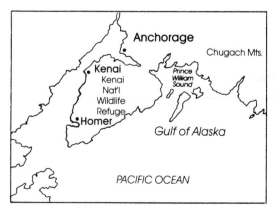

d. Now read the story and try to find the following information.

1. the name of the place where it happened
2. how long the expedition lasted
3. who is/are the main character(s)
4. what the author's main purpose was
5. what the story is about

I TOUCHED A WHALE

by Lorraine Bonney

It was 6:00 A.M., and from my sleeping bag on the shore of Prince William Sound in southern Alaska, I could hear the unmistakable sound of a whale releasing his steam into the air. I leapt up and woke up my tent mate with a shout: "Come on, Linda, there are *whales* outside!"

In minutes we were dressed and running down to the beach. We pushed our kayak, a kind of canoe-like boat, into the water and then threw in paddles and our camera bags and began to paddle into the bay. We had been waiting for this moment for seven weeks.

The whales we were looking for, the humpbacks, weigh 30 to 40 tons and can grow up to 50 feet long. I was hoping to get a prize-winning photograph of the whales. Again we heard the whales blow and then with a shout Linda pointed to a second whale about 200 yards from us.

Excited beyond words, we began to paddle closer to the two giants. It was a breathtaking sight to see the whale arch its back to dive, its tail raising high, and then diving gracefully under to feed far below. Both Linda and I were clicking away

furiously at our cameras only to discover that we hadn't focused them properly.

We paddled with all our strength to the next spot where we hoped they might be. We got as close as 75 feet but we weren't at a good angle to take the prize-winning picture I was hoping for. When next we saw the whales they were far out in the bay. We had missed our chance for this morning.

I wasn't always a whale chaser. As a matter of fact I had never been in Alaska until this trip started. My husband and I always dreamed of traveling to Alaska but we never had the chance. His death the previous year had left me lonely and depressed. An invitation from friends to join their kayaking expedition seemed the perfect answer to my sadness.

Two hours later, the whales have returned to the bay. This time I am sitting alone in my kayak waiting for them to surface, still hoping for another chance to get a prize-winning picture.

Suddenly, I hear it, the soft *swoosh* of a whale spouting out his air. And he's only 40 feet away

WHALES AND THE SEA 75

from me. He is huge and too close for the zoom lens on my camera. I hurriedly paddle my boat around and at the same time try to switch to the regular camera lens. I am in perfect position. This is wonderful. I wait for the tail to reach its highest point, with my finger at the ready on the camera button.

Suddenly there is another hissing sound like steam in my face. The viewer in my camera fogs up. It's the second whale—a great black shadow right next to my seat! He's going to capsize me!

I have no idea what to do. Instinctively my hand reaches out to the whale, as if I could possibly hold back a 40 ton giant. At one moment my hand is touching the warm rough hide, and then there is only water. I can't believe my eyes. Gracefully and carefully the whale has gone under my kayak and has disappeared.

The whale reappears 15 feet ahead of me. He dives and makes a magnificent picture but I am completely unable to do anything about it. My camera is useless. I am useless; I am in shock. Somehow I find the strength to begin to paddle back to camp.

People gather around. At first I can't speak but gradually the words come and I explain my adventure. No, I didn't get a prize-winning photograph.

But, I touched a whale.

GLOSSARY
cap·**size**—to tip over
de·**pressed**—sad
hide—outer skin
pad·dle—long flat pole or stick for making a boat move
re·**lease**—let out

Activity 2: Scanning for details

Now scan the story quickly to find the following information and write it on your paper. Then check your answers with your partner and correct them if you need to.

a. setting (place only) of story
b. time Lorraine first heard sound of the whale
c. what Lorraine did when she heard the whale
d. weight of humpback whales.
e. length of humpback whales
f. Lorraine's reason for getting near the whales
g. reason Lorraine had joined the kayaking expedition
h. what happened during Lorraine's second encounter with the whales
i. reason for being unable to take a good picture during second encounter
j. words Lorraine used to say why she was so excited

Activity 3: Understanding sequence of events—summarizing

When someone tells a story, he or she usually narrates the facts in the sequence in which they happened, that is, in chronological order. A written story, however, does not always use correct chronological order, as in the case of "I Touched a Whale." Write a summary of the story so that all the facts in it are told chronologically. Be ready to present your summary to the class.

Activity 4: Using vocabulary in context

Copy and complete each sentence on your paper, using the words in the box. Use each word only one time.

a. It's an amazing sight to see a whale . . . under the water.
b. The . . . of a whale is warm and rough.
c. The sound of the whale blowing steam into the air made Lorraine . . . out of bed.
d. When the whale was under the boat, Lorraine was sure it would . . . her.
e. Out of . . . , Lorraine tried to push the whale away.
f. The . . . sound of the whale took Lorraine by surprise.
g. Lorraine couldn't take pictures because she was in a state of . . . .
h. She paddled out into the middle of the bay in her . . . .
i. The whale swam under the boat and . . . 100 yards away.
j. . . . Lorraine recovered and got herself back to land.

capsize	dive	hide	kayak	reappeared
desperation	gradually	hissing	leap	shock

Activity 5: Reading and analyzing a short story

Look at the title of the short story on this page. Can you guess what the story will be about? Read the story and see if your guess was right.

THE VIGIL

by Jan Andrews

Along the dirt road that led through their small Newfoundland village, past the church and the schoolyard, and down onto the beach dashed Caitlin Roberts and her brother Kevin early one Saturday morning. They stopped for a moment to throw pebbles through the mist and drizzle out into the calm, gray sea.

A lock of Caitlin's long, black hair fell across her face, and as she pushed it back, her gray eyes widened.

"Kev," she cried, pointing ahead. "Look!"

What she had seen sped them on, so that within seconds they were running as hard as they could towards where a huge, black shape was lying stranded.

"A whale," Kevin called. He kicked at a broad line of small, dead fish thrown up along the high water mark as he spoke. "Must have come after the capelin."

The great creature began to thrash and churn about at their approach. Stones and sand and spray were flung up from where the outgoing tide lapped around its tail, and its body writhed and twisted, carving deep into the sea bed. Its fins flapped as if, in some dreadful way, it were trying to walk. They paused, watching in horror.

"Won't get off, will it?" Caitlin said bleakly.

Kevin shook his head. "No," he answered. "Remember, last year, up by Twillingate? There was one there. It was on TV. Folks came from St. John's even, trying to push it off. Weren't no good."

He bent, picked up a stone, weighed it on his hand, and let it drop. The whale thrashed still more desperately. Air came sighing and steaming out of its blowhole, and a long shuddering breath was sucked back in.

It seemed exhausted then. Though it eyed them warily through its tiny, deep-set eyes, it lay still. Once more Kevin took up a stone, and once more he let it drop as they went on.

They had almost reached the whale's side when they realized that, between the rocks at the cove's mouth, other whales were appearing. First one

steam spout thrust itself upward and then another; then four dark enormous shapes rose from the water, arched through the mist, and plunged.

"They come to be with it," Kevin said. "Remember Mr. Jones telling us about that in science?"

"Shh," Caitlin commanded. "Listen!"

From the blowhole of the whale on the beach a strange high sound soared. It was answered by a succession of wavering notes, and again the shapes rose, this time closer to shore. Squeaks and cries and long, drawn whistles sounded on the cold, gray morning air.

"They're talking to each other," Caitlin said in awe.

As she looked at the creature on the beach and then out into the cove she realized her cheeks were wet with tears. Glancing around, she saw that Kevin was crying, too. He wiped his hand slowly across his eyes.

"They'll stay now till it's dead, won't they?" Caitlin asked through the lump in her throat.

"Yes, Mr. Jones told all about that, too. Yes, 'course they will."

As the communication between the whales went on, Kevin perched himself against a rock.

"Will you mind, Cat?" he said at last.

"Mind what?"

"When it's dead, and Dad and the men come to cut it. There's a wonderful lot of meat on a whale."

Caitlin hung her head to let her black hair shut out her vision for a while. "Sort of," she answered quietly. "But it'd only rot and stink otherwise, like the capelin."

"What if . . . ?"

The harshness in her brother's voice made her look up quickly. His round usually cheerful face was pale and strained.

"What if what, now?" she asked.

"Well, if there'd been a gang of us, say. See, it'd have been different. We'd have yelled and laughed, and someone would've thrown a stone. Then we'd all have done it. Wouldn't have been like it is now. Not at all!"

The worry in Caitlin's gray eyes acknowledged the truth of his statement. He looked at his watch.

"Some other kid's bound to come here before long," he said. "Soon as one knows, they all will."

"We'll have to stay here then."

"We'll have to guard it."

"All day if need be."

Kevin hesitated. "Cat," he said. "We're not being daft, are we? I mean it's only an old whale and it's going to die anyway."

Doubt crept into Caitlin's mind. Already the drizzle was soaking through her jeans and running down her neck. She could feel the beginnings of cold and hunger, and fear of what the other kids in the village would say.

"I don't know," she muttered.

The whale on the beach let out another of its high strange cries, and once more the cry was answered. Brother and sister looked at each other. They knew then that they could not walk away.

"We got to, 'en't we?" Caitlin whispered.

Kevin nodded. "Yes. Yes, we have." So it was that, with Caitlin and Kevin standing by on land, and with its fellows waiting and calling to it from the sea, the whale on the beach came peacefully to the moment of its death. Gentle then was its passing; gentle and calm, like a cloud moving across the sun and breaking up and disappearing on a summer's day; certain as the tide that rose to wash cold and salt around it. For the first time, Caitlin put out a hand to touch the great body.

"The men'll come tomorrow, won't they?" she said softly. "They'll cut it. It'll be all a mess, and then nothing."

Kevin reached over and touched the dead animal, too.

"I won't be sorry we stayed," he said. "Not ever."

Caitlin took a last look out into the cove. Somehow she could feel that already the other whales were swimming past the rocks and out into the open and away.

"No more will I," she said firmly. "No more will either of us."

GLOSSARY

awe—amazement
cap•e•lin—a type of small fish
daft—crazy, silly
'ent—haven't
ex•**haust**•ed—tired
plunged—jumped in, dived
soar—to fly in the air
strand•ed—stuck on the shore, helpless
thrashed—turned, moved wildly

Answer the following questions about "The Vigil." Write on your own paper.

a. What did Caitlin and Kevin find?
b. What made Caitlin and Kevin cry?
c. Why will the men come to cut the whale?
d. Why did Caitlin and Kevin decide to watch the whale?
e. How long did the other whales stay?

Activity 6: Reacting to fiction through writing— writing an autobiographical experience

Many people are quite cruel to animals. Caitlin and Kevin make a decision to treat the whale kindly. They watch the whale to make sure that other children don't come and make noises or throw stones or bother the dying whale. They let the whale die with dignity and they feel good about it.

Write a paragraph about an experience you have had with a pet or other animal, for example, getting or finding a new kitten or puppy, losing a pet, helping an injured bird or rabbit, etc. Write about what happened between you and the animal and your feelings about the situation. Make up a story if you don't have any true-life experiences with animals.

Literary Points

Activity 1: Point of view

When discussing literature, point of view has a special meaning. *Point of view* tells who is narrating the story. *First person* point of view means that a *character* (a person) in the passage is telling the story. The character speaks of himself or herself as "I." *Third person* point of view means that the author is narrating the story. He is not a character in the story. He is outside of the story, telling the reader what is going on.

Look back in the book at the following passages; tell which point of view, first or third person, each one is written from.

Unit 2, page 11, "I'm an Advertiser"
Unit 3, page 20, "Camille"
Unit 4, page 28, "Champion Cowboy Wins Again"

Unit 7, page 53, "The Dog of Pompeii"
Unit 8, page 62, from "The Story of My Life"
Unit 10, page 75, "I Touched a Whale"

Activity 2: Reading a poem

WHALE AT TWILIGHT

by Elizabeth Coatsworth

The sea is enormous, but calm with evening and sunset,
rearranging its islands for the night, changing its own blues,
smoothing itself against the rocks, without playfulness,
    without thought.
No stars are out, only sea birds flying to distant reefs.
No vessels intrude, no lobstermen haul their pots.
Only somewhere out toward the horizon a thin column
    of water appears
and disappears again, and then rises once more,
tranquil as a fountain in a garden where no wind blows.

Reprinted with permission of Macmillan Publishing Company from DOWN HALF THE WORLD by Elizabeth Coatsworth Beston.
Copyright 1950, and renewed 1978, by Elizabeth Coatsworth Beston. Originally appeared in *The New Yorker* Magazine.

With your partner or group, decide on answers to these questions, and be ready to present your answers, together with reasons for them, to the class.

a. What time is it in the poem?
b. What is the only sign of life in the sea?
c. *Personification* is giving human characteristics to non-human things. Where does the poet use personification in the poem?
d. A *simile* is a comparison using "like" or "as." Find the simile in this poem and tell what is being compared.
e. What picture does this poem draw in your mind? How does it make you feel? What is the mood of the poem?

Looking at the Arts 11

CARLOS: Jean, I'd like you to meet George Conant, conductor of the City Opera Company, who's going to be on my show.

JEAN: It's a real privilege to meet you. I'm so glad you're going to be on Carlos's program next week.

CONANT: Well . . . most people welcome any opportunity to talk about the things that interest them. And conducting certainly interests me!

CARLOS: George, tell me . . . just what does a conductor do? I've seen you gracefully waving your conducting stick, your baton, in time to the music, but I suspect there's more to it than that! Am I right?

CONANT: You certainly are. A conductor is like the captain of a ship. You know, as conductor, I'm responsible for everything that happens during a performance. All the orchestra players and the singers watch me so that they can play together like one person. At rehearsals, one short section may be played ten or more times until it's just the way I want it to sound. In the performance, I use my baton, my eyes, and my body to help and inspire the musicians.

JEAN: Are there any special performances coming up that we should watch for?

CONANT: Well, let's see . . . right now, I'm working on a new production of *Carmen* which will be given this winter.

CARLOS: That's a Spanish opera, isn't it?

CONANT: You're right, it takes place in Spain, but it's in French. It was written by a French composer, Georges Bizet, in the 1870s, and audiences everywhere have loved it ever since.

JEAN: I'm looking forward to hearing about this new *Carmen* next week.

Communication Points
Report facts

1. **Often in writing or speaking you must assemble a group of facts and present them to others in your own words. Look at the fact sheet about *Carmen*. Then look at the paragraph which has been written from it. Notice how the facts have been put together to make a summary which can be used for a presentation.**

Carmen at the Metropolitan Opera, New York City

Fact Sheet

Name of opera: *Carmen*
Name of composer: Georges Bizet
First performance: March 3, 1875, in Paris, France
Language in which written: French
Based on work by: Prosper Merimée, French author
Brief description: A jealous lover kills his girlfriend when he finds out that she is in love with another man.

Carmen was composed by Georges Bizet. It was first performed on March 3, 1875, in Paris, France. The opera is written in French and is based on a work by the French author Prosper Merimée. *Carmen* is the story of a jealous lover who kills his girlfriend when he finds out that she is in love with another man.

2. **Use the three fact sheets below and write summary paragraphs of the facts. After you have written your paragraphs, memorize them and give them as oral reports to your partner or to the class.**

Fact Sheet 1: Book

Name of Book: *The Diary of a Young Girl*
Author: Anne Frank (1929–1945)
First published: 1947, Amsterdam
Language in which written: Dutch
Other forms in which presented: made into a movie and a play
Translations: 31 languages
Copies sold: over 5 million
Brief description: Anne Frank, a German-Jewish girl, wrote a diary as a young teenager, while she and her family were hiding from the Nazis during the Second World War. She and most of her family died in a Nazi concentration camp.

Fact Sheet 2: Musical Play

Name of musical: *West Side Story*
Written by: Leonard Bernstein, Arthur Laurents, and Stephen Sondheim
First performance: 1957, New York City
Language in which written: English
Based on work by: William Shakespeare (*Romeo and Juliet*)
Brief description: Two rival New York teenage gangs begin to fight when the leader of one gang dates the sister of the leader of the second gang; both gang leaders are killed.

Fact Sheet 3: Painting

Name of painting: German Love
Artist: Robert Indiana (American, 1928–)
First painted on canvas: 1965
Other forms: prints, posters, steel sculpture, U.S. postage stamp (1973)
Style of painting: Pop art
Brief description: Originally a painting, this design can be seen on many products.

3. **With your teacher, choose a book, painting, opera, play, or other famous work of art and write a fact sheet about it similar to those in exercise *1* above. Your teacher and your librarian can help you to find the facts for your fact sheet. Then write a summary from your fact sheet and present it as an oral report to your partner or to the class.**

Language Points

Reading fiction

1. **Before reading the story, discuss these points with a small group or with the class.**
   a. Parents often make their children do things which the parents say are "good for" the children. What sorts of things are these?
   b. How do teenagers feel about this kind of treatment from their parents?
   c. Did you ever have to tell someone some unpleasant news? What was the news? How did you feel? How did the person react?

2. **Now read the story and on your paper answer the questions that follow it.**

HAPPY BIRTHDAY, WOLFGANG MOZART

Wolfgang Amadeus Mozart

Rob had kept his promise to his parents. Piano lessons for a year, then if he didn't like them he could stop. Today was the day, glorious January 27th, exactly one year from Rob's first piano lesson. Finally he could give it up. No more lessons, no more practice in the evenings and on weekends. No more piano.

"Have you told Mrs. D'Amico about your decision, Rob?" Mrs. Begley asked.

"Have I told her? I thought you were going to tell her." Rob knew that Mrs. D'Amico needed the money she earned from giving piano lessons. She was a widow with no regular job and only a small government pension for support. He had not planned on having to break the bad news to her.

"Sorry. That's your responsibility. You're the one who doesn't want the lessons."

"Please, can't you tell her, Mom? Tell her that I've got to concentrate more on my school work, and that you forbid me to take piano any more."

"Don't be ridiculous. I want you to keep studying the piano. And even if I didn't, I wouldn't lie for you or for anyone else."

Somehow Rob knew that that would be her answer. He picked up his piano books and walked reluctantly over to Mrs. D'Amico's. Suddenly the day didn't seem so glorious. The clear sky and bright sunshine did little to cheer Rob's spirit.

He remembered that first piano lesson a year ago. He was angry at his parents for making him take the lessons. Mrs. D'Amico could tell, but she was pretending that nothing was wrong. She said happily, "*Amico* means friend in Italian. I'm Mrs. D'Amico and I'm going to be your friend. We are going to have lots of wonderful times together."

Ron doubted that a 65-year-old woman who listened to opera in her spare time would become his friend. But, as a matter of fact, over the weeks and months he had come to like her. She always had a snack for him for after the lesson, and she even told some interesting stories. Mrs. D'Amico had grown up in the neighborhood, and she told him how things had been there in the past.

"I remember when I was a girl, we used to play in a field right where your house is now. Your whole side of the street used to be farmland. Why, some people kept pigs and chickens in their back yards until about 10 years before you were born. My own father kept chickens until about 1949. I'd gather the eggs. We had one hen we called Ruth, who was just a laying fool. Sometimes we'd get five or six eggs a week from her."

Rob enjoyed talks like that, but they didn't make it worth taking piano lessons. Widow or not, interesting stories or not, he just couldn't go on with the lessons. They interfered too much with his other interests. He wouldn't even take today's lesson. He'd just tell her and go. His mind was made up. Before he could knock at the door, it was flung open by Mrs. D'Amico.

"Come in. Come in." She was happier than he had ever seen her. "I'll bet you don't know what day it is?" she asked in a teasing voice. Rob shook his head without saying a word.

"It's a day for celebrating. This is your one year anniversary. You've been playing the piano for one year now. And playing rather well, I might add. And if that wasn't enough, it's Wolfgang Amadeus Mozart's birthday. Look, I baked a cake. You know some lovely pieces by Mozart now. Perhaps we'll play them a little later."

"I don't think so, Mrs. D'Amico." Rob's heart was pounding like one of the big drums in a symphony orchestra, but he knew if he didn't tell her now, he never would.

"Come, come. You don't like Mozart? Why he's one of the most inspired composers in Western music."

"It's not Mozart. It's the piano in general. I don't like the piano, and I'm not going to take lessons any more." The words he had dreaded saying were finally out. For some reason, his heart was still pounding loudly. He was waiting for her reaction.

For just an instant there seemed to be tears in Mrs. D'Amico's eyes. But she did not cry. In a calm voice she answered, "Well, I'm sorry to hear that. I thought you enjoyed your lessons and your time here."

"I do enjoy coming here. It's just that the piano is not for me. I don't like playing music."

"What do you like?" The question was asked out of genuine interest, not in any kind of sarcastic or attacking voice.

In a rush to explain, Rob's words came pouring out like water from an open tap. "I like sports, especially soccer and swimming, and I like books. I read a lot. When I'm practicing the piano, or even sometimes when I'm playing sports, well, I'd much rather be reading."

"I see," answered Mrs. D'Amico. "Come here." Mrs. D'Amico led Rob to a room that had always been closed when he came for his piano lessons.

"This is my husband's study. It's a wonderful collection of books. Some are very rare. Some are first editions. I invite you to come over during your regular piano lesson time to use the library and read whichever books you like."

Rob smiled. Finally he felt his heartbeat begin to slow down. "I'd like that very much."

"Fine. Fine. Now let's celebrate. After all, it still is Mozart's birthday."

GLOSSARY

for·**bid**—to say no, to not allow

glor·i·ous—wonderful

pen·sion—monthly payment to retired persons or their families

pound·ing—beating

re·**luct**·tant·ly—unwillingly

sar·**cast**·ic—making fun of cruelly

spare—extra

stud·y—a small library or den

Answer these questions on your paper.

    a. Who are the main characters in this story?

    b. What are they like?

    c. The *conflict* in a short story is the basic problem that must be resolved. What is the conflict in "Happy Birthday, Wolfgang Mozart?"

    d. How is the conflict finally resolved?

    e. *Similes* are phrases that make comparisons using *like* or *as*. Find two similes in the story.

3. What do you think? Talk with your classmates.

    a. Should parents force their children to take lessons or play sports against their will?

    b. Should Rob have continued taking piano lessons rather than hurt Mrs. D'Amico's feelings?

    c. Do you think Rob will go to Mrs. D'Amico's to use her husband's books?

    d. Why does Mrs. D'Amico probably want him to keep coming to her house?

 # Reading a poem

MUSIC

by Amy Lowell

The neighbor sits in his window and plays the flute.
From my bed I can hear him,
And the round notes flutter and tap about the room,

And hit against each other,
Blurring to unexpected chords.
It is very beautiful,
With the little flute-notes all about me,
In the darkness.

In the daytime,
The neighbor eats bread and onions with one hand
And copies music with the other.
He is fat and has a bald head,
So I do not look at him,
But run quickly past his window.
There is always the sky to look at,
Or the water in the well!

But when night comes and he plays his flute,
I think of him as a young man,
With gold seals hanging from his watch,
And a blue coat with silver buttons.
As I lie in my bed
The flute-notes push against my ears and lips,
And I go to sleep, dreaming.

With your partner or a small group, discuss this poem. Consider each of the following questions, and any others that the poem may suggest to you.

1. What is the mood or feeling of the first stanza (lines 1 through 8)?
2. What is the mood or feeling of the second stanza (lines 9 through 16)? Of the last stanza?
3. How does the poet use personification in the first stanza? Does this help you to understand the feeling that the music gives her? Give reasons for your answer.
4. What are chords? Why are the "unexpected chords" in the first stanza unexpected?
5. What is the poet saying in the last three lines of the poem? Why do you think so?
6. Amy Lowell is called an "imagist" poet. What images, or pictures, does she create in this poem?
7. The poem is called "Music." In what way is its form similar to the form of a piece of music? (Think of some of the songs and other pieces of music you know.)

Listening

Listen to George Conant talking to Carlos about *Carmen*, and take notes on your paper about the following things that he says.

1. the title of the book on which the opera is based
2. the setting for the opera. (Remember that *setting* means the time and place of a story, opera, musical, play, etc.)
3. the main characters or people in the opera
4. the reason that Carmen is arrested
5. the reason that Don José deserts from the army
6. what happens at the end of the opera and why

Writing

Now make up a plot for an opera of your own. Write a short summary of the opera. Name the characters, describe the setting, and make up a dramatic situation that they are involved in. Tell what happens and how the opera ends. If you are good at music, you might even want to write a song or two that the characters might sing.

Practice Points

Turn the following passive-form sentences into the active form. Do not change the tense of the verb. If it is present tense in the passive form, it remains present tense in the active form.

The Diary of a Young Girl was written by Anne Frank.

Anne Frank wrote The Diary of a Young Girl.

1. That synthesizer is often played by a 15-year-old girl.
2. The orchestra was led last night by George Conant.
3. *Carmen* has been performed many times by the Metropolitan Opera Company.
4. The Nobel Prize for literature was won in 1930 by the American writer Sinclair Lewis.
5. *West Side Story* was recorded by Leonard Bernstein and a group of opera singers in 1985.
6. The sopranos had been asked to sing more quietly by the conductor.
7. A poem was read by Robert Frost at John F. Kennedy's inauguration as President of the United States.
8. Many famous paintings have been cleaned by the staff of the museum.
9. Not many great operas have been composed by Americans.
10. Norman Rockwell's paintings have never been approved of by serious art lovers.

Looking at Literature

Discussion Points

Discuss the following questions with your classmates.

1. Do you have a favorite author?
2. Who is it? What does he/she write about?
3. What's the difference between fiction and non-fiction?
4. Prose and poetry? Biography and autobiography?
5. What's a novel?

Herman Melville

Listening

Write the numbers *1* through *10* under each other on your paper. Then listen to the short lecture about the United States author Herman Melville and decide whether each of the following statements is true or false. If the statement is true, write *T* next to its number on your paper. If it is false, write *F*.

1. Herman Melville based many of his books on his own experiences.
2. Herman Melville sailed on a whaling ship in the South Seas.
3. Herman Melville's first novels were not successful.
4. Two of Herman Melville's novels were autobiographical.
5. All of Melville's novels were about the United States.
6. The novel *Moby Dick* was not successful when Melville first published it.
7. Captain Ahab is hunting Moby Dick because the whale once sunk his boat.
8. All members of the crew of Captain Ahab's ship are killed at the end of the novel *Moby Dick.*
9. Herman Melville also wrote poetry.
10. The point of view of the novel *Moby Dick* is third person.

Skill Points

Activity 1: Reading and analyzing literature

The passage below is taken from the opening chapter of *Moby Dick* Read it carefully. Then complete the exercises.

From MOBY DICK

by Herman Melville

Call me Ishmael. Some years ago—never mind how long precisely—having little or no money in my purse, and nothing particular to interest me on shore, I thought I would sail about a little and see the watery part of the world. . . . Whenever I find myself growing grim about the mouth; whenever it is a damp drizzling November in my soul; whenever I find myself involuntarily pausing before coffin warehouses, and bringing up the rear of every funeral I meet; [and I have to prevent myself] from deliberately stepping onto the street and methodically knocking people's hats off— then I count it high time to get to the sea as soon as I can . . . . There is nothing surprising in this. If they but knew it, almost all men in their degree, some time or other, cherish very nearly the same feelings toward the ocean with me. . . .

Now when I say that I am in the habit of going to sea whenever I begin to grow hazy about the eyes, and begin to be over conscious of my lungs, I do not mean to have it inferred that I go to sea as a passenger. For to go as a passenger you must needs have a purse, and a purse is but a rag unless you have something in it. Besides passengers get sea-sick—grow quarrelsome—don't sleep of nights—do not enjoy themselves much as a general thing—no, I never go as a passenger . . . .

No, when I go to sea, I go as a simple sailor . . . True, they rather order me about some, and make

me jump from spar to spar, like a grasshopper in a May meadow. And at first that sort of thing is unpleasant enough. It touches one's sense of honor, particularly if you come of an old established family in the land . . . And more than that all, if just previous to putting your hand in the tarpot, you have been lording it as a country schoolmaster making the tallest boys stand in awe of you. The transition is a keen one, I assure you, from a schoolmaster to a sailor, and requires a strong decoction of Seneca and the Stoics to enable you to grin and bear it. But even this wears off in time.

a. Answer the following questions on your paper.

1. Why did Ishmael first go to sea?
2. Why does he say that he goes to sea now?
3. How do you think Ishmael feels about the sea?
4. What does Ishmael say about passengers at sea?
5. How does Ishmael go to sea?
6. What kind of life does Ishmael enjoy on land? How does his life change when he goes to sea?

b. **Now take a closer look at the reading. Discuss these questions with your partner or a small group. When you have decided on your answers, write them on your paper.**

1. Find the words that Ishmael uses to tell that he is sad or depressed after being on land for too long. Are these phrases conversational English or figures of speech? Which figures of speech can you identify?
2. Ishmael loves the sea and states that all men (people) feel the same about it. Do you? Tell why or why not.
3. What kind of character is Ishmael? Is he likable! Does he have a sense of humor about himself? What words or phrases tell you so?
4. The *mood* of a piece of writing is the feeling the author creates and the reader feels. What is the mood of this passage?

c. **Listen to the lecture about Herman Melville again (*Listening*, page 88) or read a short biography of him in an encyclopedia. Find several similarities between Herman Melville and Ishmael. Write a paragraph describing how the character Ishmael and the author Melville are alike.**

Activity 2: Reading and writing about processes

When we talk about literature, we are talking about the world of books. There are many kinds of books. *Moby Dick* is one kind, a novel, that is, a long story that is made up by the author. Helen Keller's *The Story of My Life*, is another kind, an autobiography, the story of a person's life written by the person. Another kind of book is the kind you are reading right now, a textbook or schoolbook.

The photos on this page and the next one show how one textbook (one of the earlier books in this series) was printed. Look at the photos and read the captions. Then do the exercises that follow them.

a. Reum is making up a "form" of eight pages. The pages are photographic film. Black and white pages have one piece of film. Color pages have four pieces.

b. A.J. is making a metal printing plate from Reum's film. He is developing it with chemicals just as a photographer develops a picture.

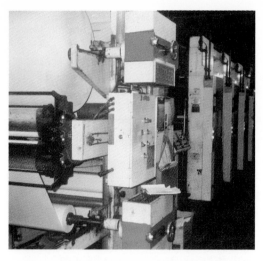

c. The printing plates go on cylinders in the printing press. There is a cylinder for each color, red, blue, yellow, and black. Other colors are mixtures of these.

d. The pressman compares the first printed sheets with the original paintings for the illustrations. He can adjust the ink on each cylinder to change the colors.

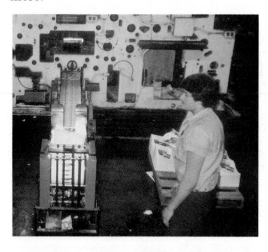

e. The press prints sixteen pages at a time and folds them. We call each group of sixteen pages a "signature."

f. This binding machine "gathers" the signatures together in the right order. The 128-page book has eight signatures.

g. Another machine puts covers on the books and glues them in place.

h. The trimming machine cuts off the edges of the books. Then workers pack the books in cartons.

1. **The photos show how this printer makes the books. As you can see, each person and each machine has a particular job to do. Write a short paragraph to explain the different steps in making these books. Use the passive form of the verbs when you can. Start like this.**

First forms of eight pages are made using photographic film. Then metal printing plates are made from the film.

2. **Many things have to happen to a book before it can be printed. A compositor sets type on a computer keyboard. Artists draw or paint the illustrations. Photo researchers find the photographs or hire photographers to take them. A color separator makes the four pieces of film for each color picture. A designer shows where all the type and illustrations go on each page.**

   Write another paragraph, using the passive form of the verbs, that tells about these steps. Use such time signal words as *before, after, then.*

3. **Work in groups of four or five people. Think of other processes, for example, the various steps involved in making a car, producing a movie, or building a house. Discuss the steps with your classmates. Then write a paragraph for each of the processes you want to describe. If necessary, use an encyclopedia and/or other reference books.**

Activity 3: Reading and interpreting a short story

Read the following short story. Then answer the questions.

THE LETTER FROM AMERICA

I

George Kyrykos listened while Mr. Stavros read him the letter from his brother. George smiled happily at his brother Stratis's success in America. Stratis had left their town near Patras only three years ago, in 1914, and already he was part-owner of a small restaurant in New York City. He even spoke some English. His children were able to read and write. Irene, his eldest daughter, had written this letter. Yes, Stratis had done well, and he hadn't forgotten his family in Greece.

The last part of his letter proved that point. Mr. Stavros read, "Some day we will have the money and room to bring you and Sophie to come live with us, dear brother, but now it is not possible. However, we do have room for Nikolas. His cousins miss him terribly, and so do his loving aunt and uncle. Send him to us so that he can benefit from the education and opportunities in America. My love to all. Affectionately, your brother, Stratis."

George was unprepared for his brother's request. He sat quietly for a moment. Finally Mr. Stavros interrupted his thoughts. "It will be difficult to send the boy away, George?"

"For me, and also for his mother. I'm not sure we can do it."

Mr. Stavros said, "Now would be a good time. We are no longer neutral. We have entered the war, and it seems to get only bigger and bloodier. Send the boy soon, if you are going to send him. The war will not end soon; there may not be another good time."

"Thank you, Mr. Stavros, for your time, and for your advice. Will you be able to write my reply to my brother when we have decided?" asked George.

"Yes, of course. But remember, George, as soon as possible," answered Mr. Stavros.

George placed a coin on Mr. Stavros's desk and left the room. The cool sea air of the evening kissed his face as he walked back to the small home where he lived with his wife, Sophie, and his son, Nikolas.

II

"Never! Never!" The words flew out of Sophie's mouth like poison arrows. "Our only son! Oh, George, how could you even consider it? I couldn't bear to be apart from him, to never see him again. You ask too much of me!"

"Do you think I want to send him away?" cried George. "He does a man's work on our fishing boat. He is no longer the little boy who bothers his father for a ride on the boat or for a childish job to keep him busy. He is almost my equal in work, and my companion. Sending him away is like sending away my right arm. I do not *want* to send him away, but I feel that we must."

"Yes, yes, I know. The bright future . . . America . . . success and the streets lined with gold," Sophie wailed, wringing her hands in distress. "But what about the past? Our traditions, our songs, our language. He will forget them all . . . and maybe us as well."

George tried to comfort her. "You are being too dramatic, Sophie. We are sending him to my brother—to Stratis and Effie. They will raise him properly, as you and I have done all these years. Our ways are in his head and in his heart. He could never forget such a loving mother as you. I guarantee it."

Sophie began to cry. "I'm not sure, George, I'm just not sure."

George was not sure either. A part of him believed all of Sophie's arguments. His own love for his son made the decision even more difficult. But Mr. Stavros's talk of war made it seem as if he had to decide to send Nikolas away at once. Why should he believe Mr. Stavros? Others said the war would end soon. George blew out the lamp and let the arguments chase each other in his head. He was unsure of what he would write back to his brother.

III

"So am I to be sent away to America?" Nikolas had spoken very little the next morning at home and waited to say these words until he and his father were far out at sea.

George laughed. "So you were awake last night while your mother and I were discussing your fate?"

"Didn't you always say I had a wolf's hearing?" joked Nikolas.

"Yes, it's true. There were never any secrets from you. You always seemed to be able to discover our secrets. And we were never able to hide a birthday present from you either, my big-eared son." George reached over and patted his son's shoulder.

"Our small house helps, too!" said Nikolas with a laugh.

"Well, what's your opinion?" asked George. "That is the most important opinion of all, really."

"I want to go, Father," said Nikolas. "I love you and Mother, and our life here. But I want more—I want to be able to learn about so many things. Maybe I will be a fisherman in America, too, but maybe I can do other things. You know that here I will not have any choice." Nikolas looked at his father with worry in his eyes. "I want to get you and Mother to America before the war comes to our town."

George watched the waves slap against the boat for a moment. "So, it's settled. You go to your uncle in America."

Nikolas asked, "What about Mother? And how will you manage the fishing without me?"

George answered, "There will be many tears, but your mother will understand. And I will find a boy to help me on the boat."

Nikolas nodded. He and his father stood in silence for a moment until the screech of seagulls raiding their fishing nets startled them both.

George pulled on the end of the net. "Right now there are fish to catch. You haven't gone to America yet! Let's get to work."

GLOSSARY
ar•gu•ments—reasons
dra•**ma**•tic—emotional
in•ter•**rupt**—to break in when someone else is talking, thinking, or doing something
neu•tral—not on either side, uncommitted
raid•ing—attacking
re•**quest**—to ask
screech—to yell
set•tled—decided
star•tled—surprised

---

a. **Understanding the story: answer the questions on your paper.**

1. What does Stratis offer in his letter?
2. Why does Mr. Stavros advise George to make a quick decision?
3. Why doesn't Sophie want Nikolas to go to America?
4. What are George's reasons for and against Nikolas going to America?
5. How did Nikolas find out about his uncle's offer?
6. What was Nikolas's decision? Why did he make that decision?

b. Analyzing the story: discuss the questions with your partner or a small group. When you have decided on your answers, write them on your paper.

1. As you know, the *setting* of a story tells the time and place when it is happening. What is the setting of this story and why is it important to the final outcome of the story?
2. The *conflict* in a story is the major problem that must be resolved. What is the conflict in this story?
3. How is this conflict resolved?
4. Why did George go to see Mr. Stavros? What information does that give you about George? Why does he leave Mr. Stavros a coin?
5. You remember that the *mood* of a story is the feeling that the author is trying to communicate. Which of the following words best describes the mood of this story?

    solemn   dull   hopeful   comical

6. *Point of view* tells who is narrating the story. Is "A Letter from America" told from a first or third person point of view?

Literary Points
Activity 1: More about personification

You'll remember that *personification* gives human qualities to inanimate (non-living) objects. Writers use personification, and all figures of speech, to make their ideas more real for readers.

You're going to analyze the use of personification in some sentences. You're going to tell what the human qualities are that the author has given to objects. Then you're going to rewrite the sentence in ordinary language. Look at the following sentence.

The flowers put on their best dresses to attend Mother Nature's spring ball.

Now look at the way the sentence has been analyzed.

Human qualities: The flowers are given the human qualities of being able to dress themselves and go to a party.
Ordinary language: Flowers look pretty in the springtime.

Analyze each of the sentences below in the same way. On your paper write the human qualities given to the objects, and then rewrite the sentence in ordinary language.

a. The train crawled pitifully into the station, its engine crying out, "Help! Help!"
b. The next-door neighbor's music invaded our apartment and tore us from sleep.
c. This good old car has been faithful to me for the last ten years.
d. The gentle sun smiled on the fields and encouraged the plants to grow.
e. The cold attacked the weary travelers with its icy knife and sent chills through their bodies.
f. The rain danced joyously on the rooftops and then jumped daringly to the ground.
g. The old elevator groaned miserably as yet another shopper entered its tiny space.
h. Luck entered the room and whispered the winning lottery numbers into Mrs. Garcia's ear.

Activity 2: Reading a poem

What ocean or sea are you closest to?
Have you ever seen the ocean or sea during a storm? What does it look like?
Here is one poet's idea.

THE SEA

by James Reeves

The sea is a hungry dog,
Giant and gray.
He rolls on the beach all day.
With his clashing teeth and shaggy jaws

Hour upon hour he gnaws
The rumbling, tumbling stones,
And "Bones, bones, bones, bones!"
The giant sea-dog moans,
Licking his greasy paws.

And when the night wind roars
And the moon rocks in the stormy cloud,
He bounds to his feet and snuffs and sniffs,
Shaking his wet sides over the cliffs,
And howls and hollos long and loud.

But on quiet days in May or June,
When even the grasses on the dune
Play no more their reedy tune,
With his head between his paws
He lies on the sandy shores,
So quiet, so quiet, he scarcely snores.

© James Reeves Estate. Reprinted by permission of the James Reeves Estate

a. What does the author compare the sea to in this poem?
b. How does the author personify the sea? (What life-like actions does the author give the sea?)
c. What two different kinds of sea does the author describe?
d. When is the sea not like a hungry dog?
e. What words rhyme in this poem?
f. Compare this poem with *Whale at Twilight* (page 80). How are the two poems alike? How are they different?
g. The author uses many words that have the sound of what they are describing (onomatopoeia). Some of those words are: *clashing, rumbling, moans.* See how many other such words you can find in the poem.

13 SPECIAL EFFECTS

CARLOS: It's interesting to see how they make a person seem to fly in a commercial. I always used to wonder how they worked some of the special effects in the movies I watched. Now Chris is being flown right here in the studio!

JEAN: Flying is one of the easier effects, actually. It's used all the time. It's all done with wires.

CARLOS: Why can't the wires be seen on the screen?

JEAN: Notice that they're blue like the background. They blend right in.

ANNE: Ready? Now, I want to see him really flying! And I want to hear the wind blow all the time during this scene.

ROY: No problem.

ANNE: Are you all set with the shot of New York?

ROY: All set. It's going to be projected on that screen to the right.

ANNE: Okay! Let's fly!

ROY: It's working perfectly! Look at SuperChris flying!

ANNE: And you can really hear the wind blowing! Terrific!

CARLOS: It's very exciting! Thanks for letting us watch!

Communication Points

Describe actions

1. Read these sentences from the dialogue on page 98.

I want to *see him* really *flying!* We can *see SuperChris* really *flying* now. And you can *hear the wind blowing* from behind.	I want to *hear the wind blow* all the time during this scene.

Notice the two kinds of sentences in the box. Read the following paragraph and find sentences or phrases of these two kinds. Make two columns on your paper and write each sentence or phrase in the appropriate column.

Yesterday afternoon I was looking out the window when I saw a very unusual bird landing on the windowsill. I stayed there for about five minutes, watching the beautiful red and yellow bird hop around and wondering what kind of bird it was. Then I heard my brother singing in the next room. I like to hear my brother sing, but yesterday I got very upset. You want to know why? Well, the bird heard my brother singing and flew away. I could see its wings fluttering as it took off from the windowsill. I still didn't know what kind of bird it was. I ran to get my bird book, yelling at my brother while I ran. "I wanted to hear that bird sing, not you!" He saw me looking everywhere for the book. He laughed at me, saying, "That was a red and yellow flycatcher, Maria. You can tell from the feathers sticking out on top of its head." But I think he was just kidding me.

Use your lists to ask and answer questions with your partner. Use questions such as the following.

a. What did the person see?
b. What did the person watch?
c. What happened next?

> A: What did the person see?
> B: She saw a very unusual bird landing on the windowsill.
> A: What did the person watch?
> B: She watched the beautiful red and yellow bird hop around.

2. Use the following phrases to make a story. On your paper, make the phrases into sentences and put them in a logical order. Add any details you want to make your story interesting.

. . . saw the men hanging onto the ropes
. . . looked up at the men cleaning the windows on the fifth floor
. . . people yelled, "Hang on, we're coming!"
. . . saw something moving on the side of the building
. . . watched the firemen race up the ladders and catch the men
. . . heard the fire engine siren screaming
. . . walking along Harrison street
. . . saw the men come down the ladder safely
. . . heard someone yell "Help!"
. . . standing on a platform held by ropes at each end
. . . saw the ladders going up the side of the building
. . . saw the hook and ladder truck come racing around the corner
. . . one rope was broken

Describe repeated actions

1. **Make a chart on your paper like this. Then fill in the chart for yourself (or your parents). Use** *once/twice/three times,* **etc.,** *a week/month/year* **or** *Never.*

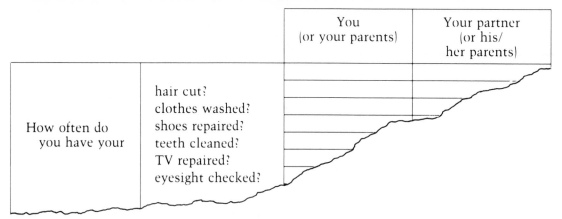

		You (or your parents)	Your partner (or his/ her parents)
How often do you have your	hair cut? clothes washed? shoes repaired? teeth cleaned? TV repaired? eyesight checked?		

Now ask and answer the questions with your partner.

> A: How often do you have your hair cut?
> B: Once a month.

2. **Now ask and answer these questions with your partner. Use the same form as shown in the box. Then change roles.**

> A: Why are you going to the photographer's studio?
> B: I want to have my passport photo taken.

a. Why is Sue going to the beauty parlor?
b. Why is Joseph going to the dry cleaner?
c. Why are they going to the shoe repair shop?
d. Why are you going to the dentist?
e. Why is Kim going to the eye doctor?
f. Why is Juan going to the tailor?
g. Why are you going to the hospital?
h. Why is the teacher going to the photocopier?
i. Why is Jeanne going to the auto mechanic?
j. Why are Judie and Al going to the watch repair shop?

Language Points
Reading about entertainment

SPECIAL EFFECTS IN THE MOVIES

Motion pictures, or movies, are actually a series of still pictures. Each still picture, or frame, isphotographed on a long reel of film and then pro-jected on a screen. The pictures are photographed and projected at the rate of 24 frames per second to create the illusion of continuous motion.

This continuous movement is the basic illusion of the movies. There are many other illusions, however, and they are created through the use of special effects. With special effects, movies show us superheroes who can fly, monsters that eat whole cities, and space creatures from far-off planets. Special effects add interest and excitement to many movies.

One very basic special effect is the use of frame-by-frame photography. Each frame is photographed individually. Then it is projected as if it were part of a continuous movement. Animated cartoons are made this way. And models of mons-

King Kong on the Empire State Building

ters can be moved slightly between frames. When the frames are projected at 24 frames per second, the monsters seem to move by themselves.

Another basic special effect is the use of models, paintings, and drawings, which are photographed so that they look real. Movies and TV programs that look as if they were photographed in a jungle, on an island, or in the desert may actually be photographed in a studio, with background paintings, photographs, or models designed to look like the real thing. Using small models and frame-by-frame photography, spaceships can be made to collide and dinosaurs to fight each other.

Then there is composite photography. Images photographed at different times can be combined to move together as if they had been photographed together. One actor can portray twin brothers talking to each other, for example.

The use of stunt persons or "doubles" is not a true special effect but it helps in creating an illusion. Stunt persons are professional men and women who have trained themselves to drive fast cars, leap from tall places, run from (or into) burning buildings, and do any number of dangerous things that most actors are unwilling or unable to do. Stunt persons look like and dress like the actors whom they are replacing. When we see the real actor in closeups before and after the "stunt," we have the illusion that that actor actually did it.

One other basic technique that movie producers use to create illusions is to put into a continuous sequence film that was shot at different times. For example, you may see passengers enjoying themselves in a railroad car, then see the train smashing into another train, then see the passengers crying out in pain in the wrecked car. It all happens in quick sequence, but in fact the director will shoot it as three separate scenes, perhaps on separate days. The accident itself may be photographed using models, or it may be real trains with stunt persons or dummies in them. The wrecked railroad car is a separate set, built to look as nearly as possible like the interior of the car in the first scene.

Many directors are famous for their "special" special effects. Alfred Hitchcock was a pioneer in using special effects to make horror movies even more terrifying. Other more recent directors who are famous for using special effects are Steven Spielberg, George Lucas, and Dino Di Laurentis. All of these directors understand that the movies are a world of illusion, and that the illusion can be heightened by the careful use of special effects.

GLOSSARY
com·**pos**·ite—made up of separate parts
dum·mies—mannequins, human-size dolls
il·**lu**·sions—ideas or impressions not connected with fact
pi·o·**neer**—one of the first persons to do a thing
pro·**ject**·ed—shown on a screen
se·ries—a group of things coming one after another

Use the information in the article to answer these questions on your paper.

1. What is a frame?
2. How many projected frames per second create the illusion of continuous movement?
3. What is the special effect used to make animated cartoons?
4. What is composite photography?
5. Who was one of the first directors to use special effects in horror films?
6. Who are some of the modern-day directors who are famous for their special effects?

Working with the dictionary

Many words have more than one meaning. Use a dictionary to find the different meanings for the words below, all of which are used in "Special Effects in the Movies" which you have just read. On your paper write all the meanings for the word as given in the dictionary and underline the one which shows how it is used in this reading. NOTE: Some of these words are listed in the dictionary as both nouns and adjectives or as nouns, adjectives, and verbs. Give only the meanings for the part of speech shown here: noun (*n*), adjective (*adj*) or verb (*vi* or *vt*).

frame (n)	interest (n)	shoot (vt)	stunt (n)
image (n)	run (vi)	still (adj)	train (n)

Writing

You are going to write a review of a movie or television program you have seen recently. Write about what was good or bad about what you saw. Before writing, talk with your classmates, friends or parents about the movie or program. Write down as many ideas as possible, including those you get from others. Then write a first draft. Be ready to share this first draft with your partner or the class, and listen to any criticism or suggestions they may have. Consider these suggestions and criticisms when you write your final draft. Be especially careful to correct any errors in spelling and grammar. And of course, use your best handwriting.

In your review be sure to include as much of the following information as you can.

name of the film or program
names of the leading actors
name of the director
length of the film or program
setting (time and place of the action)

main characters
special effects you noticed
brief account of the story
your opinion of the film or
   program (how good or bad it was)

Listening

You will hear a person talking about an experience he has recently had. Listen carefully and take as many notes as you can on your paper.

Then talk to your partner and try to reconstruct the complete story. Try to remember as many details as you can. Write a first draft of the story as well as you can remember it.

After you have written the story, listen again to the person telling it. Compare what you have written with the original, and correct your draft. Then write a final draft of the story in your own words.

Practice Points

1. **Imagine that you have just seen a movie which used a lot of special effects. Match each phrase in column A with a phrase in column B to make sentences that tell what you saw and heard. Write the sentences on your paper.**

A	B
a. We saw the city	k. circling the city.
b. You saw the people	l. growing to gigantic proportions.
c. We saw the planet	m. landing in the desert
d. I heard the lions	n. wrapping themselves around the actors' necks.
e. We heard the tornado	o. changing its shape.
f. I saw the planes	p. roaring in the jungle.
g. We saw the spaceship	q. screeching as the cars slowed.
h. You heard the brakes	r. blowing across the open plain.
i. I saw the snakes	s. running out of the building.
j. We saw the ants	t. shining with a strange light.

2. **Copy and complete these sentences on your paper. Choose any verbs that fit the meaning, and use the right verb form. Use only one word in each blank. Use your imagination to make your answers interesting and fun!**

   a. We . . . the small boat . . . the ocean shore.
   b. Yesterday, as I opened the curtains in the morning, I . . . an old man . . . toward Rupert Street.
   c. All I remember is that I . . . something on my leg and then I fell down.
   d. When I . . . the meat . . . , I remembered that I had forgotten to turn off the oven.
   e. When I came home last night, I could . . . somebody . . . down the stairs.
   f. When I . . . somebody . . . against the door of the bus I shouted, but it was too late.
   h. The game on TV was very exciting, and I could . . . all the family . . . every move of the players.
   h. I . . . somebody . . . "Stop that!" and then there was silence.

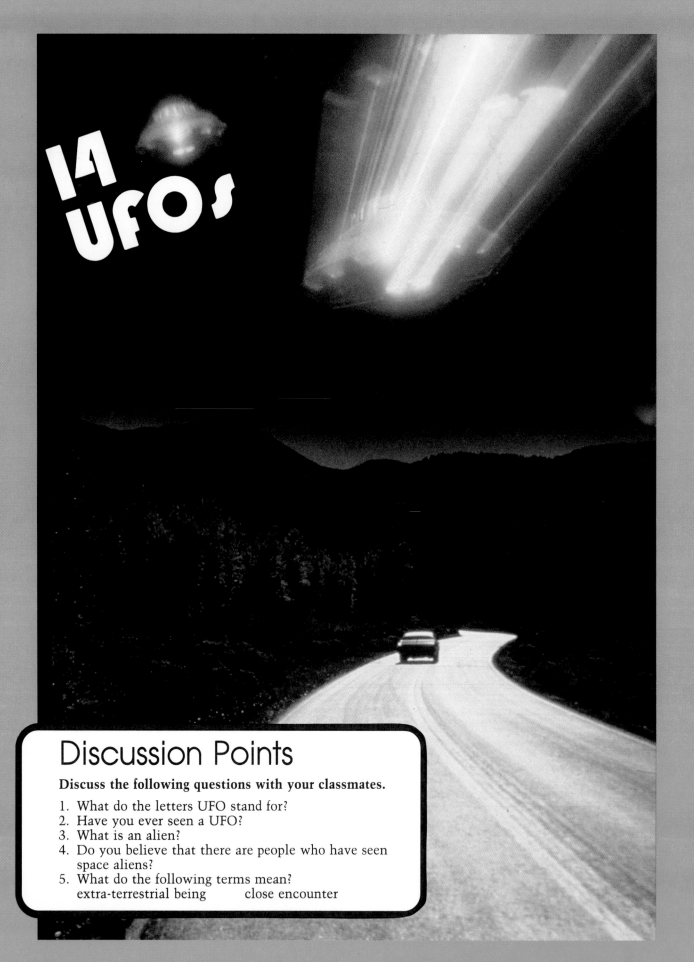

14 UFOs

Discussion Points

Discuss the following questions with your classmates.

1. What do the letters UFO stand for?
2. Have you ever seen a UFO?
3. What is an alien?
4. Do you believe that there are people who have seen space aliens?
5. What do the following terms mean?
   extra-terrestrial being   close encounter

Listening

Listen to the lecture about mistaken UFO sightings. Take notes on your paper so that you can identify each of the following objects.

1. the bright planet most often mistaken for a UFO
2. three man-made objects often confused with UFOs
3. the colors of airplane lights at night
4. the shape clouds can take when they pass over hills
5. lights shooting across the sky
6. the familiar heavenly object which is responsible for 5% of all UFO sightings

Skill Points

Activity 1: Learning familiar abbreviations

An abbreviation is a short series of letters that stands for a longer word or series of words. There are many different kinds of abbreviations. One kind that is often used in the United States is made by taking the initial or first letters of the words in the name of something and putting them together. An example is UFO, which stands for Unidentified Flying Object.

On your paper, match these abbreviations with the things they stand for. If you know, or can guess them, write also the words that the letters stand for.

1. VCR
2. MPH
3. RN
4. BA
5. FBI
6. RPM
7. RSVP
8. MD

a. a request for an answer placed at the bottom of an invitation
b. a physician or surgeon
c. a machine to play video tapes
d. the number of revolutions or turns that a motor makes in a minute
e. a government organization that fights crime in the United States
f. how fast an automobile or airplane moves
g. a degree or diploma awarded after four years of college
h. a person who takes care of sick people under the direction of a doctor

After you have completed the activity, turn to page 106 to check your answers.

Activity 2: Acronyms

Another kind of abbreviation like those in activity 3 is the acronym. An acronym is a word made up of letters from the name of an organization or thing. Acronyms are pronounced as words, not as a series of letters. One familiar acronym that came out of World War II is <u>radar</u>. Radar is made from the term <u>ra</u>dio <u>d</u>etecting <u>a</u>nd <u>r</u>anging.

Match these acronyms with the things they describe.

1. NASA
2. REO
3. SMOG
4. SONAR
5. NATO
6. LASER
7. MADD
8. SEATO

a. <u>m</u>others <u>a</u>gainst <u>d</u>runk <u>d</u>riving; an organization to keep people from driving while drunk
b. <u>s</u>ound <u>n</u>avigation <u>a</u>nd <u>r</u>anging: a system used to locate things underwater
c. <u>l</u>ight <u>a</u>mplification by <u>s</u>timulated <u>e</u>mission of <u>r</u>adiation; narrow beam of light used in surgery
d. <u>R</u>obert <u>E</u>. <u>O</u>lds; old car named after its maker
e. <u>N</u>ational <u>A</u>eronautics and <u>S</u>pace <u>A</u>dministration
f. <u>N</u>orth <u>A</u>tlantic <u>T</u>reaty <u>O</u>rganization
g. <u>sm</u>oke and f<u>og</u> mixed together
h. <u>S</u>outh<u>e</u>ast <u>A</u>si<u>a</u> <u>T</u>reaty <u>O</u>rganization

New acronyms are constantly being made. With your partner list other acronyms that you know and where they come from. Look at the names of gasoline companies, foods, and political groups. Make up some acronyms of your own.

Activity 3: Reading for information

You have probably seen many stories about UFOs. Some of these stories are obviously products of people's imaginations. Stories with headlines like the two below are not to be taken seriously.

Aliens kidnaped me and took me to Mars!

I was married to a being from outer space!

There are some stories about UFOs that are more believable, however. The following article describes a real experience. Read it and answer the questions that follow it.

AIRWAY INTRUDERS

"It's approaching from the east," the young Australian pilot reported on the radio. "It appears to be flying over me at a speed I can't identify . . . . It's passing me now . . . It has an oblong shape. Now it's coming back. It has a green light."

This was the beginning of the strange events that took place in the sky south of Melbourne on a quiet night towards the end of 1978. The pilot, Frederick Valentich, went on reporting, "The object's just over me now . . . . My engine's misfiring . . . . It's gliding, but it isn't a plane . . . ." The transmission stopped at that point and the aircraft disappeared without leaving any traces. It probably sank in the dark waters of the ocean. This is the only reported sighting that has ended up tragically in the history of UFOs.

But that was not the end of the story. During the following days, many unidentified bright objects were seen in the sky over Australia and New Zealand. On December 31, 1978, a TV troupe was flying from Wellington to Christchurch in New Zealand. At about midnight, they saw some strange lights. The lights appeared and disappeared continuously and were brighter than any other object in the sky. At the same time, the operators in Wellington spotted some inexplicable radar images. One of the objects seemed to be chasing the aircraft. The people on board the plane reported that one of the lights got as near as ten miles. It had a very bright base, and a kind of transparent sphere on top. The sighting lasted more than 15 minutes. The objects were filmed by the TV cameraman who was able to shoot 23,000 frames on 16 mm film.

The film was sent to the United States Navy for computer analysis. It revealed a series of mysterious flying objects. A sequence showed a bell-shaped object that glowed in its lower part, as it had been described by the cameraman. Another sequence showed an object that shifted from a bright white circular shape into an orange triangular shape. The American optical physicist Bruce Maccabee, who did the analysis, estimated that if the object was really at a distance of ten miles from the aircraft it had a diameter of between 20 and 30 meters. Its light was equivalent to the light of a huge 100,000 watt bulb. The speed of one of the objects reached 5,000 kilometers per hour while it was looping the loop.

When Bruce Maccabee had completed his study, the film, together with the evidence collected, was sent to a group of American scientists. They were experts in various fields such as astronomy, biophysics, radar, and optical physiology. The scientists were unanimous in declaring that they were not able to explain any of the strange events that had occurred that night in New Zealand. The lights could be neither stars or meteors, nor stratospheric balloons or reflected lights. They were UFOs, that is Unidentified Flying Objects. This was the first and only sighting in which UFOs were seen, filmed and signaled by radar equipment at the same time.

Reprinted with permission of Educational Development Corporation.

Work with your partner to answer these questions. Be prepared to present your answers to the class.

a. A tragic event is something that is very sad. What was tragic about Frederick Valentich's encounter with the UFO?
b. Over what countries did the UFOs appear?
c. How did the camera crew describe the UFO they saw?
d. What information did the American Navy analyst provide about the UFOs after looking at the film?
e. What was the conclusion of the group of scientists to whom the film was sent?
f. What about the camera crew's sighting of the UFO was different from any other UFO sightings?

Literary Points

Activity 1: Hyperbole

Hyperbole (exaggeration) is a figure of speech. It may be used in a serious way, but it is often used for casual speech or for humor. The exaggeration is so great that no one takes the statement for a true fact.

a. Here are some examples of hyperbole. Read each one and then tell or write on your paper why it is hyperbole.

1. I'm dying of thirst.
2. He's so tall he can touch the sky.
3. These mosquitoes are killing me.
4. My new sweater cost a fortune.
5. My hand's so tired it's about to fall off.
6. I must have walked a thousand miles today.
7. Your chocolate chip cookies are the best in the world.
8. I ate too much—I'm so full I'm going to burst.

b. Now you try some. See if you can create five examples of hyperbole, statements that are very exaggerated—for effect or to be funny. Write your examples on your paper.

Activity 2: Reading a Poem

Read the poem about a visitor from outer space. Then answer the questions.

SOUTHBOUND ON THE FREEWAY

by May Swenson

A tourist came in from Orbitville,
parked in the air, and said:

The creatures of this star
are made of metal and glass.

Through the transparent parts
you can see their guts.

Their feet are round and roll
on diagrams—or long

measuring tapes—dark
with white lines.

They have four eyes.
The two in the back are red.

Sometimes you can see a 5-eyed
one, with a red eye turning

on top of his head.
He must be special—

the others respect him,
and go slow,

when he passes, winding
among them from behind.

They all hiss as they glide
like inches, down the marked

tapes. Those soft shapes,
shadowy inside

the hard bodies—are they
their guts or their brains?

**Work with your partner to answer these questions. Be prepared to present your answers
to the class.**

a. Look at the title of the poem. What is a freeway?
b. What does the "tourist" see on the freeway?
c. What does the "tourist" think the things he/she/it sees on the freeway are?
d. What are the "feet" of the creatures in reality?
e. What are the eyes?
f. What is the 5-eyed creature the tourist describes?
g. How do the 4-eyed creatures act around the 5-eyed creatures?
h. What are the soft shapes inside?

Activity 3: Reacting to poetry through writing

**Imagine that you meet a space creature who has just landed on Earth. She wants to
know about life here. She wants to know: what human beings eat, how they
communicate, if life is peaceful here, what human beings do for work and play, and what
scientific breakthroughs have been accomplished. Write a composition which expresses
your ideas on these topics so that you are explaining them to a visitor from another
planet. Discuss your ideas with your classmates before you begin writing. Write down all
your ideas and then make a first draft. Share your first draft with your teacher and
classmates before completing a final draft. Include any grammatical or other corrections
that your teacher may have suggested in your final composition.**

Volunteers at Work (15)

JEAN: We're here in Danford today to learn about its unique training program for volunteer firefighters, and to meet Harvey Stone, the man who directs it. Welcome to Channel 8, Harvey.

HARVEY: It's a pleasure. And let me welcome you to the Danford firehouse on training night. One evening a week, this group gets together to train to be volunteer firefighters.

JEAN: Are they paid for this?

HARVEY: No, they're all volunteers.

JEAN: How old are they?

HARVEY: They're all between 16 and 18.

JEAN: What do they do here? Do they study?

HARVEY: Not really. They practice actually doing the things that firefighters do. Take those kids over there. They're trying to connect fire hoses as fast as they can.

JEAN: It looks hard.

HARVEY: It is. If they had connected the hoses more quickly, they wouldn't have wasted so much water.

JEAN: Do they always work in teams like that?

HARVEY: Yes, they do. That's very important. They have to learn how to work together and to learn from their mistakes. Isn't that right, Joe?

JOE: It sure is. Take just now. If we had pulled the hose up to the hydrant right away, the other members of the team would have gotten water on the fire much faster. We know that now, and we'll do it right next time.

JEAN: I'm really impressed with the way you train these young people, Harvey.

HARVEY: We try hard. After all, they're going to be our firefighters in the years to come.

JEAN: And they'll be the best! I can see that. Thanks for talking with Channel 8, Harvey.

HARVEY: You're welcome, I'm glad you came.

Communication Points
Ask and talk about hypothetical past situations

1. **Read the dialogue again with your partner and find the mistake that the young firefighters made during their training session. On your paper write the sentence that tells about the mistake.**

2. **Link the half sentences below to make complete logical sentences. Write these complete sentences on your paper.**

   a. If you had walked up to me,
   b. If the weather had been good yesterday,
   c. If the three kids had connected the hose right away,
   d. If we had played better last Saturday,
   e. If the bus hadn't broken down,
   f. If I had studied when I was in school,
   g. If you had helped me yesterday,
   h. If I had had a lot of money,
   i. If you had invited me to your party,

   j. I would have bought a yacht.
   k. we would have won the game.
   l. I would have finished my homework earlier.
   m. they wouldn't have wasted so much water.
   n. I would have said, "Hello!"
   o. I would have a better job now.
   p. I would have come.
   q. I would have gone to the beach.
   r. we would have gotten there on time.

3. **Now use the sentences you made to ask and answer with your partner. Then change roles.**

   > A: What would you have done if I had walked up to you?
   > B: I would have said, "Hello!"

4. **Ask and answer with your partner about five or more hypothetical past situations, that is, things that could have happened but did not happen.**

   > A: What would you have done if you hadn't passed the test?
   > B: I would have studied harder and asked to take it over again.

Request others to do things

Students have volunteered to clean up the Community Center. Look at the list of tasks on the next page. Then work in groups of three. Students ask about the tasks and assign them to others in the group. Then change roles.

> A: What would you like (Student C) to do?
> B: Please tell her to wash the windows on the second floor.
> A: Okay, I'll tell her. (Student C), would you please wash the windows on the second floor?
> C: Sure, I'd be glad to./No, I'm sorry, I'm already busy. But I could ask someone else to do it.

> A: Do you want (Student C) to sweep the entrance hall?
> B: No, would you ask him to empty all the wastebaskets?
> A: Okay, I'll ask him. (Student C), I'd like you to empty all the wastebaskets.
> C: I'd be happy to./Oh, I've already emptied them!

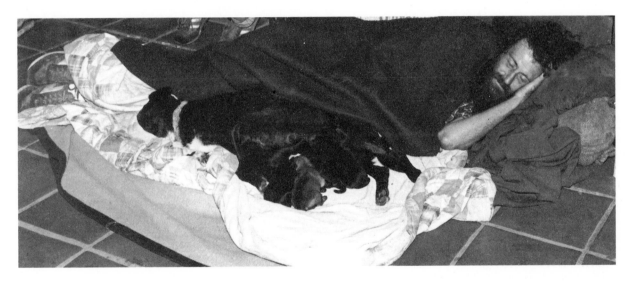

Tasks
replace the burned out light bulbs
sweep the entrance hall
wax the floor in the meeting room
wash the windows on the second floor
wash the tables in the lunch room
vacuum the carpet in the office
empty all the wastebaskets
clean the stove and the refrigerator

Language Points

Reading about people

Read about the way that one 12-year-old volunteer was able to affect the lives of hundreds of people. Then answer the questions.

THE GOOD THAT LIES WITHIN THE HUMAN HEART

Not long ago, Trevor Ferrel was a 12-year-old boy living in a middle-class suburb of Philadelphia, one of the large cities of Pennsylvania, in the northeastern part of the United States. One December night, he heard a newscast about the problems of the hungry and homeless in Philadelphia which shocked him. Like so many young people who live in comfortable, middle class surroundings, Trevor had no idea that not many miles away there were hundreds and hundreds of people who had no homes, no food, no money, and almost no possessions except the clothes on their backs.

Trevor asked his parents how he could help these people. He wanted to know where they were and what could be done. Mr. and Mrs. Ferrel weren't sure what could be done, but they did know where to find the homeless of Philadelphia. They decided to drive Trevor into the city so that he could see the streets where the homeless congregated, warming themselves on the heat that came up from the subway.

The young boy did not go empty-handed. He brought a spare pillow and blanket with him. Trevor gave these things to the first homeless person he saw. The man was delighted with the

Trevor Ferrel with the Philadelphia City Council

gifts, and Trevor was pleased with the idea of helping a fellow human being. He couldn't wait to do it again the next night.

The following morning, Trevor and his parents searched the house for other unused clothing and blankets. That night they were back on the streets of Philadelphia, giving out their supplies to those most in need.

Within a couple of days, however, there was nothing left to give. The Ferrels had given away all the supplies they could. But Trevor was not ready to give up and forget about the homeless people he was just getting to know. He made up flyers, handbills that explained what he was doing for the homeless and what his needs were. His phone number was printed on each one. Trevor distributed these around the neighborhood and went home to wait for the response.

The response was overwhelming. People were glad to give the food, blankets, and clothing that Trevor had asked for. Local stores and restaurants also donated supplies for Trevor's cause. Many individuals even offered their time. This was important. The extra workers helped Trevor and his parents prepare and distribute the food and supplies. Soon the Ferrels' van was well known on the Philadelphia streets. For many of the men and women on the streets that winter, it meant survival.

The homeless people were not the only ones who noticed Trevor's efforts. Soon television stations, newspapers, and magazines were talking and writing about the 12-year-old who was helping the homeless. Donations began to pour in from all over the country. Trevor and his parents used the money to buy more supplies for the homeless. A local Philadelphia church donated a 30-room house in the city of Philadelphia. This became the base of operations for Trevor's distribution to the homeless.

To reward him for all he had done, the Philadelphia City Council passed a resolution proclaiming Trevor Ferrel to be "an example of the good that lies within the human heart."

Trevor deserved that proclamation. He had shown what one person, even one who was only 12 years old, could do.

GLOSSARY

con·gre·gat·ed—got together

de·**light**·ed—pleased, happy

do·**nat**·ed—gave

emp·ty **hand**·ed—having nothing

fly·ers—papers with information or advertising on them

hand·bills—papers with information or advertising on them

home·less—people without a place to live

spare—extra

sub·urb—city or town outside of a larger city

On your paper, answer these questions about "The Good that Lies Within the Human Heart." Be sure that you are telling the reason why in each answer, and not just restating the question.

a. Why was the news of homeless and poor people so shocking to Trevor Ferrel?
b. Why did Trevor want to help other homeless people after helping the first person he saw?
c. Why did Trevor have to ask his friends and neighbors to help?
d. Why was extra help important?
e. Why did donations start to come in from all over the country?
f. Where does the title of the story come from? What do you think it means?

Writing

What could you do to change things? What problems do you see in your neighborhood, your city, your state, or the world? Write a composition about what you would do to solve one or more of these problems and make things better. Before writing, talk with your classmates, friends, or parents about this topic. Write down as many ideas as possible including those you get from others. Then write a first draft. Share this first draft with your partner, a small group, or the class and your teacher. Listen to any suggestions or criticisms they may have. Consider these suggestions or criticisms when you write your final draft and be especially careful to correct any errors in spelling or grammar. Of course you will use your best handwriting or typing for your final draft.

Listening

Listen to the lecture about youth groups and the volunteer work that they do. Take notes on your paper so that you can make a chart that lists the name of each organization and the volunteer activities each has participated in.

ORGANIZATION	ACTIVITIES

Practice Points

1. **Rewrite these sentences on your paper using the correct form of the verb in parentheses. Notice that all the sentences are about hypothetical past situations, that is, things that could have taken place in the past but did not. Look at the examples, and notice that the verbs in the rewritten sentences are in the past perfect tense.**

   If you (wear) your sweater, you wouldn't have been cold.

   If you had worn your sweater, you wouldn't have been cold.

   If you had studied for the exam, you (not + fail) it.

   If you had studied for the exam, you wouldn't have failed it.

   a. If you (drive) carefully, you wouldn't have had the accident.
   b. If she (not + leave) her umbrella at home, she wouldn't have gotten wet.
   c. If you had gotten up on time, you (not + miss) the train.
   d. If the manager (talk) to me that way, I would have left his office immediately.
   e. If you had turned the oven off, you (not + burn) the roast beef.
   f. If he hadn't bumped into that car, the police (not + catch) him.
   g. You would have lost a couple of pounds if you (run) for two miles every day last summer.
   h. If you (have) a good breakfast this morning, you wouldn't have been so hungry at lunch.
   i. John (not + be) late for school this morning if he had not gone to bed late last night.
   j. I (buy) that car if I had had enough money.

2. On your paper, copy and complete the second sentence in each pair so that it has the same meaning as the first sentence in the pair.

He didn't speak to you because he didn't see you. If he had . . .

If he had seen you, he would have spoken to you.

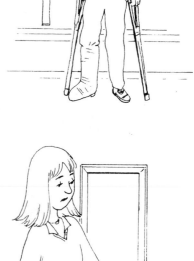

a. I didn't phone Mary because I didn't know her telephone number.
   If I had known Mary's telephone number . . . .
b. He knows so much about cars because he's been a mechanic all his life.
   If he hadn't . . . .
c. The manager didn't inform me about the situation because he didn't see me.
   If the manager . . . .
d. I had the accident because I didn't wait for the "walk" sign.
   If I had . . . .
e. The dog ate all the meat because John didn't close the kitchen door.
   If John . . . .
f. Last year I didn't go to the Bahamas on vacation because I didn't have enough money.
   If I had . . . .
g. Carlos had an argument with Barbara last night and he was in a bad mood this morning.
   If Carlos hadn't . . . .
h. They didn't understand what the teacher said because they talked all the time.
   If they hadn't . . . .
i. Bill lost his job because he was late every morning.
   If Bill hadn't . . . .
j. I answered the phone because I didn't know it was Peter.
   If I had . . . .

SCIENCE FACT/ 16
SCIENCE FICTION

Discussion Points

Discuss the following questions with your classmates.

1. What is a fact?
2. What is fiction?
3. What is an opinion?
4. Name some of the planets.
5. What is a solar system? a galaxy? the universe?
6. Do you think there is life on other planets or in other galaxies
7. Why or why not?
8. Do you think man will fly to other galaxies in the next 100 years?
9. Which of the answers to the questions above are facts? Which are opinions?

Listening

1. **Carlos, Jean, and Barbara are having a discussion about their favorite science fiction authors. Listen to the conversation and answer the following questions.**

   a. Who is the science fiction writer that Carlos likes best?
   b. What about Jean? Who does she prefer?
   c. Does Barbara like the same authors? Does she prefer somebody else?
   d. What is Jean's favorite book?
   e. What is Barbara's favorite book?

2. **Now listen again, and then read the statements below. Decide if each statement is a fact or an opinion. Remember that a *fact* is something you can check or prove. An *opinion* is something that someone thinks or believes but that cannot be checked or proved. Write your answers on your paper.**

   a. opinion

   a. Jules Verne's stories of adventure are exciting.
   b. Ray Bradbury is the best of the 20th century science fiction writers.
   c. Isaac Asimov writes essays as well as science fiction.
   d. H. G. Wells is the author of *The Time Machine*.
   e. H. G. Wells is a better writer than Jules Verne.
   f. Jules Verne wrote his stories in French.
   g. Ray Bradbury is too moralistic in his writing.
   h. Jules Verne is sometimes called the father of science fiction.
   i. Isaac Asimov's writings are so easy that anyone can read them.
   j. Ray Bradbury has written many novels as well as short stories.

Skill Points

Activity 1: Reading non-fiction—sequence, cause and effect

Read the passage below, then complete the exercises.

THE SUN'S FUTURE

Helium-burning stage

The sun is made up mainly of the gases hydrogen and helium. Scientists predict that our sun has a life expectancy of ten billion years. They say that the sun is now about five billion years old. When the sun gets to be ten billion years old, it will go through many changes.

In the first stage, the sun will have burned up all its hydrogen. This will cause the structure of the sun to change. The core or center will shrink and the surface will expand or grow larger. As the sun expands it will become cooler, change color and become red. At this stage the sun is called a red giant. As a red giant the sun will be 100 times brighter than it is right now.

In the next stage the sun will begin to burn its helium. The sun will continue to expand. During the first helium-burning stage it will become 50 times larger than its present size. There will be a rapid rise in the sun's temperature. The planets closest to the sun, Mercury, Venus, the Earth, and Mars, will be destroyed.

As the helium burns, the sun will grow larger and larger until it is 400 times its present size. At this point the large, more distant planets of Jupiter, Saturn, Uranus, Neptune, and Pluto will change dramatically. Unlike the closer planets, however, they will not be destroyed.

When all the nuclear energy of the sun (the energy bound up in the material of the sun) is burned up, the sun will collapse. It will shrink and become a white dwarf—a very small dim star. A white dwarf shines only because it has a small amount of gravitational energy left in it. (Gravitational energy comes from the pull of large bodies toward each other or toward smaller bodies.)

Stars in formation

The sun will change again when that small amount of gravitational energy has burned up. It will become a black dwarf—a dead star with no light or heat. All of this is billions of years away according to scientists. By that time the population of the Earth may have moved on to other solar systems or galaxies.

a. **Sequence: On your paper, rewrite the stages of the sun listed below in correct chronological order according to the article.**

> white dwarf stage
> helium burning stage
> black dwarf stage
> red giant stage
> hydrogen burning stage

b. **Cause and effect: Match the cause in column A with its most direct effect in column B. Write the answers on your paper.**

A	B
a. Sun burns up all its hydrogen.	h. Temperature rises rapidly.
b. Core of sun shrinks.	i. Sun becomes a black dwarf.
c. Sun begins to burn helium.	j. Inner planets are destroyed.
d. Sun's temperature rises.	k. Structure of sun changes.
e. Sun grows to 400 times its present size.	l. Sun's surface expands and temperature gets lower.
f. All sun's nuclear energy is used up.	m. Outer planets change dramatically.
g. Sun's gravitational energy is used up.	n. Sun collapses and becomes a white dwarf.

Activity 2: Using reference books to complete an assignment

Reference books, like the dictionary and encyclopedia, give specific information about topics of interest to their readers. Reference books are loaded with facts, and contain very few if any opinions. You will probably need a dictionary or encyclopedia to complete the exercise below where you are required to match common scientific terms in column A to their meanings in column B.

Palomar Observatory Photograph

Write your answers on your paper.

1. constellation – h.

A	B
1. constellation	a. the path in space along which a heavenly body moves
2. atmosphere	b. one who studies the stars and heavens
3. lunar	c. the relative brightness of a star
4. gravity	d. a star that suddenly flares up or fades away after a period of time
5. magnitude	e. having to do with the moon
6. nova	f. an odorless gas which is lighter than air
7. galaxy	g. the movement of a planet around a sun or of any other satellite around its center of attraction
8. helium	h. any group of stars imagined to represent the outline of a being or thing, usually mythological
9. astronomer	i. any of several hundred smaller planets between Mars and Jupiter
10. asteroid	j. one of billions of systems, each including stars and other matter, that make up the universe
11. meteor	k. a smaller body attending upon or revolving around a larger one
12. satellite	l. the body of gases surrounding the Earth or any other celestial body
13. orbit	m. the act or state of turning, as on an axis
14. revolution	n. the attraction of large bodies, such as the earth, moon, planets, etc. for smaller bodies near them
15. rotation	o. a piece of matter moving through space which, on entering Earth's atmosphere, heats up and appears as a streak of light across the sky

Activity 3: Reading science fiction

THE HAUNTED SPACESUIT

by Arthur C. Clarke

When Satellite Control called me, I was writing up the day's progress report in the observation bubble—the glass-domed office that juts out from the axis of the space station like the hubcap of a wheel.

It was not really a good place to work, for the view was too overwhelming. Only a few yards away I could see the construction teams performing their slow-motion ballet as they put the station together like a giant jigsaw puzzle. And beyond them, twenty thousand miles below, was the blue-green glory of the full Earth, floating against the raveled starclouds.

"Station supervisor here," I answered. "What's the trouble?"

"Our radar's showing a small echo two miles away, almost stationary, about five degrees west of Sirius. Can you give us a visual report on it?"

Anything matching our orbit so precisely could hardly be a meteor. It would have to be something we'd dropped—perhaps an inadequately secured piece of equipment that had drifted away from the station. So I assumed; but when I pulled out my binoculars and searched the sky around Orion, I soon found my mistake. Though this space traveler was man-made, it had nothing to do with us.

"I've found it," I told Control. "It's someone's test satellite—cone-shaped, four antennas. Probably U.S. Air Force, early 1960s, judging by the design. I know they lost track of several when their transmitters failed. There were quite a few attempts to hit this orbit before they finally made it."

After a brief search through the files, Control was able to confirm my guess. It took a little longer to find that Washington wasn't in the least bit interested in our discovery and would be just as happy if we lost it again.

"Well, we can't do that," said Control. "Even if nobody wants it, the thing's a menace to navigation. Someone had better go out and haul it aboard; get it out of orbit."

That someone, I realized, would have to be me. I dared not detach a man from the closely knit construction teams. We were already behind schedule, and a single day's delay on this job cost a million dollars. All the radio and TV networks on Earth were waiting impatiently for the moment when they could route their programs through us, and thus provide the first truly global service, spanning the world from pole to pole.

"I'll go out and get it," I answered, and though I tried to sound as if I were doing everyone a great favor, I was secretly not at all displeased. It had been at least two weeks since I'd been outside.

The only member of the staff I passed on my way to the air lock was Tommy, our recently acquired cat. Pets mean a great deal to men thousands of miles from Earth, but there are not many animals that can adapt themselves to a weightless environment. Tommy mewed at me as I clambered into my spacesuit, but I was in too much of a hurry to play with him.

At this point, perhaps I should remind you that the suits we use on the station are completely different from the flexible affairs men wear when they want to walk around on the Moon. Ours are really baby space ships, just big enough to hold one man. They are stubby cylinders, about seven feet long, fitted with low-powered propulsion jets, and have a pair of accordion-like sleeves at the upper end for the operator's arms.

As soon as I'd settled down inside my very exclusive space craft, I switched on power and checked the gauges on the tiny instrument panel. All my needles were well in the safety zone, so I gave Tommy a wink for luck, lowered the transparent hemisphere over my head and sealed myself in. For a short trip like this, I did not bother to check the suit's internal lockers, which were used to carry food and special equipment for extended missions.

As the conveyor belt decanted me into the air lock, I felt like an Indian papoose being carried along on its mother's back. Then the pumps brought the pressure down to zero, the outer door opened, and the last traces of air swept me out into the stars, turning very slowly head over heels.

The station was only a dozen feet away, yet I was now an independent planet—a little world of my own. I was sealed up in a tiny, mobile cylinder, with a superb view of the entire universe. But I had practically no freedom of movement inside the suit. The padded seat and safety belts prevented me from turning around, though I could reach all the controls and lockers with my hands or feet.

In space, the great enemy is the Sun, which can blast you to blindness in seconds. Very cautiously, I opened up the dark filters on the "night" side of my suit, and turned my head to look out at the stars. At the same time I switched the helmet's external sunshade to automatic, so what whichever way the suit gyrated my eyes would be shielded.

Presently, I found my target—a bright fleck of silver whose metallic glint distinguished it clearly from the surrounding stars. I stamped on the jet control pedal and felt the mild surge of acceleration as the low-powered rockets set me moving away from the station. After ten seconds of steady thrust, I cut off the drive. It would take me five minutes to coast the rest of the way, and not much longer to return with my salvage.

And it was at that movement, as I launched myself out into the abyss, that I knew that something was horribly wrong.

It is never completely silent inside a space suit; you can always hear the gentle hiss of oxygen, the faint whir of fans and motors, even, if you listen carefully enough, the rhythmic thump that is the pounding of your heart. These sounds reverberate through the suit, unable to escape into the surrounding void. They are the unnoticed background of life in space, for you are aware of them only when they change.

They had changed now; to them had been added a sound which I could not identify. It was a muffled thudding, sometimes accompanied by a scraping noise.

I froze instantly, holding my breath and trying to locate the alien sound with my ears. The meters on the control board gave no clues. All the needles were rock-steady on their scales, and there were none of the flickering red lights that would warn of impending disaster. That was some comfort, but not much. I had long ago learned to trust my instincts in such matters; it was their alarm signals that were flashing now, telling me to return to the station before it was too late . . .

Even now, I do not like to recall those next few minutes. Panic slowly flooded into my mind like a rising tide. I knew then what it was like to face insanity; no other explanation fitted the facts.

For it was no longer possible to pretend that the noise disturbing me was that of some faulty mechanism. Though I was in utter isolation, far from any other human being or indeed any material object, I was not alone. The soundless void was bringing to my ears the faint, but unmistakable, stirrings of life.

In that first, heart-freezing moment it seemed that something was trying to get into my suit—something invisible, seeking shelter from the cruel and pitiless vacuum of space. I whirled madly in my harness, scanning the entire sphere of vision around me except for the blazing, forbidden cone towards the Sun. There was nothing, of course. There could not be—yet that scrabbling was clearer than ever.

Despite the nonsense that has been written about us, it is not true that spacemen are superstitious. But can you blame me if, as I came to the end of logic's resources, I suddenly remembered how Bernie Summers had died, no further from the station than I was at this very moment?

It was one of those "impossible" accidents; it always is. Three things had gone wrong at once. Bernie's oxygen regulator had run wild and sent the pressure soaring. The safety valve had failed to blow—and a faulty joint had given way. In a fraction of a second, his suit was open to space.

I had never known Bernie, but suddenly his fate became of overwhelming importance to me, for a horrible idea had come into my mind. One does not talk about these things, but a damaged space suit is too valuable to be thrown away, even if it has killed its wearer. It is repaired, renumbered—and issued to someone else . . .

What happens to the soul of a man who dies between the stars, far from his native world? Were you still here, Bernie, clinging to the last object that linked you to your lost and distant home?

As I fought the nightmares that were swirling around me—for now it seemed that the scratchings and soft fumblings were coming from all directions—there was one last hope to which I clung. For the sake of sanity, I had to prove that this wasn't Bernie's suit—that the metal walls so closely wrapped around me had never been another man's coffin.

It took me several tries before I could press the right button and switch my transmitter to the emergency wave length. "Station!" I gasped, "I'm in trouble! Get records to check my suit—"

I never finished; they say my yell wrecked the microphone. But what man, alone in the absolute isolation of space, would not have yelled when something patted him softly on the back of the neck?

I must have lunged forward, despite the safety harness, and smashed against the upper edge of the control panel. When the rescue squad reached me a few minutes later, I was still unconscious, with an angry bruise across my forehead.

And so I was the last person in the whole satellite relay system to know what happened. When I came to my senses an hour later, all our medical staff was gathered around my bed, but it was quite a while before the doctors bothered to look at me. They were much too busy playing with the three little kittens our badly misnamed Tommy had been rearing in my space suit's Number Three storage locker.

GLOSSARY

al·ien—foreign
coast—to move without effort
de·**cant**·ed—poured or emptied out
de·**tach**—to take away, to unhook or remove
drift·ed—sailed away
glint—to shine
gy·rat·ed—turned, whirled
haul—drag
is·sued—given to
juts—sticks or points out
launched—sent out or forward
lunged—pushed, sent forward
men·ace—threat, problem
me·ters—dials, measuring devices
muf·fled—deadened, as sound
pa·**poose**—baby carried on its mother's back
rear·ing—bringing up, raising

re·**paired**—fixed
re·**ver**·ber·ate—to make a hollow sound or echo
sal·vage—something rescued
span·ning—crossing, reaching from one end to the other
stub·by—short, fat
su·**perb**—great, wonderful
su·per·**sti**·tious—believing in things that are not based on scientific fact or reason
thrust—forward movement
un·**con**·scious—not awake or aware
ut·ter—complete, total, absolute
vac·u·um—empty space without air
whirled—turned around rapidly, spun
wrecked—broken, hurt

---

a. **Understanding the story: answer the following questions on your paper.**

1. Why does the astronaut leave the ship?
2. Who is Tommy?
3. What is the astronaut's spacesuit like?
4. What did the astronaut hear inside his space suit?
5. Who was Bernie Summers?
6. What was the astronaut's fear about his spacesuit?
7. Why did the astronaut want to get records to check his suit?
8. What happened to the astronaut?
9. What was in his suit?
10. Why was Tommy misnamed?

b. Now take a closer look at the story. Discuss these questions with your partner or a small group. Then write your answers on your paper.

1. Point of view identifies the narrator's voice as either first or third person. What is the point of view in "The Haunted Spacesuit?"
2. Setting is the time and place of a story. What is the setting of "The Haunted Spacesuit?"
3. Why do pets mean a great deal to astronauts?
4. What was the effect on the astronaut when he heard a muffled scraping sound coming from his spacesuit?
5. What warned him to return to the station?
6. Do you feel that the astronaut in the story believes in other life forms? Find information from the story to support your opinion.
7. What was the astronaut's assumption about the cause of the noise in his spacesuit? Was he right or wrong?
8. What caused the astronaut to scream into his microphone?
9. How did he get back to the space station?

Literary Points

Activity 1: Writing science fiction

Science fiction stories usually take place in the future on distant planets or in far-off galaxies. These stories often include robots, computers, amazing inventions, and space creatures in addition to the normal everyday humans we are used to in regular fiction. In science fiction almost anything is possible.

One of the most important parts of science fiction writing—or any writing for that matter—is the story. Something interesting or exciting must happen to make the story or novel worth reading. It's not enough for a writer to just write about space creatures and computers on another planet; there must be an interesting plot or story-line.

Write a science fiction short story about one of the following ideas:

a. landing on a planet where other life already exists
b. a battle between computers and humans where the computers want to take over the world
c. a time machine which can send you back into the past or forward into the future
d. the last days on Earth before the sun gets too hot and consumes the planets closest to it

Activity 2: Word study—idioms

An *idiom* is a group of words which have a special meaning as a group. The meaning of each word by itself does not add up to the same meaning as that of the group. For example,

roll with the punch = don't be discouraged when things go wrong

The phrase came from the sport of boxing, where a boxer who is hit tries to move away with the punch, to make the blow weaker.

On your paper, choose the right meaning from column B to go with the idiom in column A. The answers are at the bottom of the page.

	A		B
a.	you're driving me out of my mind	f.	feel out of place
b.	got out of bed on the wrong side	g.	give away a secret
c.	have a crush on someone	h.	think you're in love
d.	be a fish out of water	i.	be irritable
e.	let the cat out of the bag	j.	bothering me

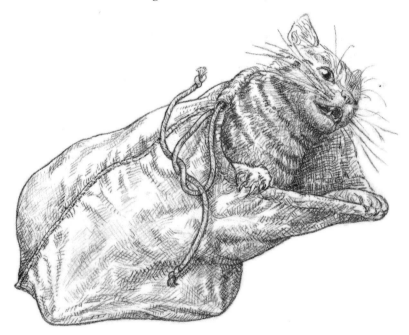

Checkpoints

Unit 1

Has	Steve had his photograph taken?	Yes, he's already had it taken.
	Diane applied for her passport?	No, she hasn't applied for it yet.

Is	Bob Chang	the one who likes	making model airplanes?
	Sheila Beattie		to shop for other people?

Unit 3

Why should I	watch the news? get the car ready?

So that	you can see if	there any signs of hurricanes.
In case	you have to	leave in a hurry.

How much rain	is expected?
The hurricane watch	has been changed.

Unit 5

She lives in Woodside. Koko uses sign language.	She said that Dr. Patterson lived in Woodside. The book said that Koko used sign language.

I plan to run for Congress. Who are you? Do you live here?	He said he planned to run for Congress. She asked him who he was. She asked her if she lived there.

Unit 7

If	you leave	Boston at 8:15	you'll be	in Chicago at 9:15.
	you don't leave		you won't be	
Unless	you leave			

If Sinath follows his plan, will he	travel to Europe	before after	he graduates from high school?
	work part time	as soon as	

Unit 9

What would you do	if you were	lost in the woods? in the desert?

If I was	lost in the woods in the desert	I'd . . . .

What should I get for a present?

If I were you I'd get . . . .

No, I'd rather get . . . .

Unit 11

Carmen	was composed	by	Georges Bizet.
Diary of a Young Girl	was written		Anne Frank.

Unit 13

You can hear the wind	blow. blowing.
She saw the bird	hop. landing.

I want to have	my hair cut. my picture taken.

Unit 15

If you had	walked up to me, helped me yesterday,	I would have	said "Hello." finished my homework.